The Fall of the
Luftwaffe in Colour
Battle of Britain, 1940

CLIVE J. M. ELLIS

KEY
Books

Acknowledgements

In this book are the best quality images from a large variety of international sources. I take this opportunity to express my gratitude to the following individuals who have helped me caption, and assisted me in collating, such a collection over the past 20 years. These fellow enthusiasts and authors include Eddie Creek, Simon Parry, Peter Cornwell, Tony Holmes, Dave Wadman, Eric Mombeek, Kent Battle of Britain Museum Trust, Bob Collis, Melvin Brownless and the late Michael Payne, Ken Watkins, Pat Burgess and Steve Hall.

Many thanks to all who have encouraged and supported me.

ABBREVIATIONS (abbreviations in brackets)

Luftwaffe Crew

Flugzeugführer (Ff) – Pilot

Beobachter (Bo) – Observer

Bordfunker (Bf) – Wireless operator

Bordmechaniker (Bm) – Flight engineer

Bordschütze (Bs) – Gunner

Luftwaffe Ranks

Hauptmann (Hptm) – Flight lieutenant

Oberleutnant (Olt) – Flying officer

Leutnant (Lt) – Pilot officer

Oberfeldwebel (Ofw) – Flight sergeant

Feldwebel (Fw) – Sergeant

Unteroffizier (Uffz) – Corporal

Obergefrieter (Ogefr) – Leading aircraftman

Gefrieter (Gefr) – Aircraftman 1st class

Published by Key Books
An imprint of Key Publishing Ltd
PO Box 100
Stamford
Lincs PE19 1XQ

www.keypublishing.com

The right of Clive J. M. Ellis to be identified as the author of this book has been asserted in accordance with the Copyright, Designs and Patents Act 1988 Sections 77 and 78.

Copyright © Clive J. M. Ellis, 2020

ISBN 978 1 913295 83 7

Typeset by Aura Technology and Software Services, In

Contents

Foreword 4

Introduction 5

Chronology 6

Chapter 1 July...10

Chapter 2 August 15

Chapter 3 September...48

Chapter 4 October 84

Bibliography 96

Foreword

So many books have been written on the subject of the epic aerial struggle known as the Battle of Britain in 1940 that many might question the need for another tome on the subject. However, this work, using an extraordinary combination of stunning colourised images and extensively researched text, provides us with a new and different perspective on the battle between 'the few' and Hitler's vaunted Luftwaffe.

In close collaboration with the author, Ghermán Mihály has assisted transforming these images from traditional monochrome. Some of the photos are well known, others more obscure, but all are part of the history of this famous air campaign which changed the course of the war. This fresh approach has ploughed an entirely new furrow across the Battle of Britain genre. Set out in date order, and complimented by detailed descriptions, these images accurately portray the stark reality of the desperate days in 1940 when Britain stood alone. Here, for the first time, is a colour rendition of the Luftwaffe's Eagles in defeat.

The county of Suffolk (1939–45) in particular is my area of specialist interest so it is very appropriate to highlight such 1940 events that otherwise get a rare mention in published material for this period. Luftwaffe crashes documented within the boundary of Suffolk amount to around 14 for the whole of 1940. Similarly, within close proximity (i.e. only a few miles outside the Suffolk/Essex border) up to an additional 11 can be mapped as well. I'm therefore glad to say Clive has succeeded in managing to bring to light a few here and rightfully put us on the map where we belong!

Bob Collis
Aviation Historian and Archivist
Lowestoft, Suffolk, 1 November 2018

Introduction

2020 is the 80th anniversary of the Battle of Britain, to which this book is dedicated. It essentially follows the air war over the UK from early July 1940 to early November 1940 when Operation *Sealion*, the planned German invasion of England, was poised ready to go and all that remained was for the Luftwaffe to sweep the RAF from the skies so the invasion could begin. During those crucial four months, the Luftwaffe began, in dominant form, traversing the waters that surround the British Isles with ease. However, what began to emerge is that at the height of the battle, and despite multiple large incoming raids at any one time, the RAF fighter pilots were a force to be reckoned with and the Germans found that the loss rate of their aircrew was too great.

Meticulously researched over the course of 20 years, this collection of some of the best classic photographs of 'downed' enemy aircraft, from July to November 1940, has been painstakingly colourised, giving the rare spectacle of new colour from the Battle of Britain period. The study of the Luftwaffe's camouflage and markings is a complex subject, compounded by the general lack of quality colour photographs. Inevitably, therefore, most photographs appearing here were black and white to begin with. From this point, the author has adopted his own interpretation of the contemporary colours adopted by various units on the timeline; whilst of course it is recognised that some may at times contradict those opinions. To help redress the balance, some previously unseen/unpublished images are produced in original colour too.

The images are complimented by information, sometimes in note form, about the aircraft, personnel and action involved in the incident. A summary table is included which details the chronology of events for quick reference. In all cases, the author has endeavoured to describe the Luftwaffe's planes as far as documented facts will allow. At the beginning of the war, the RAF were already well prepared for intelligence gathering and had established teams to collate details about the Luftwaffe's equipment, systems and organization. There were two separate departments for this purpose: AI1(g), which was responsible for information about the aircraft, engines and weaponry; and AI1(k) which interpreted information concerning the Luftwaffe's organizational structure and its personnel. Many of the details given in this book have been taken from information collected by these departments. It should also be noted that some entries are shorter than others as either the information simply isn't out there, or in some cases is already heavily documented in plenty of other well-known publications.

Chronology

Date	Aircraft	Werknummer	Location	Aircraft Code	Unit
08 07 40	Bf 109 E-3	1162	Bladbean Hill, Elham, Kent	4+	4./JG 51
11 07 40	Bf 110 C-4	3551	Grange Heath, near Lulworth, Dorset	2N+EP	9./ZG 76
12 07 40	He 111 P	-	Horse and Jockey Inn, Hipley, near Southwick, Hants.	G1+FA	5./KG 55
21 07 40	Bf 110 C	2177	Goodwood Home Farm, Chichester, W Sussex	5F+CM	4(F)./14
24 07 40	Bf 109 E-1	6296	North Down, Broadstairs/Margate, Kent	<I+I	Stab III./JG 26
28 07 40	Ju 88 A-1	7036	Buckholt Farm, Sidley, Bexhill, E Sussex	9K+HL	3./KG 51
08 08 40	Ju 87 B	5600	St. Lawrence, near Ventnor, lsle of Wight	S2+LM	4./StG 77
11 08 40	Ju 88 A-1	-	Blacknor Fort, Portland, Dorset	B3+DC	Stab II./KG 54
12 08 40	Bf 110		Missing in action (lost at sea)	2N+AN	8./ZG 76
12 08 40	Ju 88 A-1	3134	Horse Pasture Farm, Westbourne, near Emsworth, W Sussex	9K+EL	3./KG 51
12 08 40	Bf 109 E-1	3367	Berwick rail crossing, Mays Farm, Selmeston, E Sussex	14+	2./JG 52
12 08 40	Bf 109 E-1	-	Hengrove, near Margate, Kent	<-+	III./JG 54
13 08 40	Do 17 Z	-	Stodmarsh, N Kent	U5+ER	7./KG 2
13 08 40	Bf 109 E-1	5068	New Salts Farm, Shoreham, W Sussex	<+	1./JG 2
13 08 40	Do 17 Z	-	Seasalter mudflats, near Whitstable, Kent	U5+DS	8./KG 2
13 08 40	Do 17 Z	-	Railway, Pherbec Bridge, Barham, Kent	U5+KA	S./KG 2
13 08 40	Ju 88 A-1	-	Great Ham Farm, Earnley, near Selsey, W Sussex	L1+BS	8./LG 1
15 08 40	Bf 110 C		Weymouth Bay, Dorset	2N+BC	Stab III./ZG 1
15 08 40	Ju 88 A	-	Priors Leaze, near Woodmancote, W Sussex	L1+SM	4./LG 1
15 08 40	Ju 88 A	-	Great Ham Farm, Earnley, near Selsey, W Sussex	L1+FM	4./LG 1
15 08 40	Bf 110 C-6	-	Broadbridge Farm, Smallfield, near Horley, Surrey	S9+TH	1./ErpGr 210
15 08 40	Bf 110 D	3339	School Farm, Hooe, E Sussex	S9+CB	ErpGr 210
15 08 40	Bf 110 D	3338	Bletchlinglye Farm, Catts Hill, Rotherfield, E Sussex	S9+AB	ErpGr 210
15 08 40	Bf 110D	3341	Hawkhurst, Kent	S9+CK	2./ErpGr 210
15 08 40	Bf 109E-4	1910	Lightlands, Frant, E Sussex	3+	ErpGr 210

Date	Aircraft	Werknummer	Location	Aircraft Code	Unit
16 08 40	Ju 87 B-2	5580	Selsey Rd, Church Norton, W Sussex	T6+HL	3./StG 2
16 08 40	Ju 87 B-1	5618	Bowley Farm, South Mundham, W Sussex	T6+KL	3./StG 2
16 08 40	He 111 P	1582	Honeysuckle Lane, High Salvington, Worthing, W Sussex	G1+FR	7./KG 55
16 08 40	Bf 110 C-4	3278	Droke near Upwaltham, East Dean, W Sussex	2N+CC	Stab II./ZG 1
16 08 40	He 111 P	2217	Maudlin Farm, Steyning Bowl, W Sussex	G1+HP	6./KG 55
18 08 40	Do 17 Z-2	334	'Sunnycroft', Golf Road, Kenley, Surrey	F1+HT	9./KG 76
18 08 40	Do 17 Z-2	-	Leaves Green, near Biggin Hill, Kent	F1+DT	9./KG 76
18 08 40	Bf 110 C	3102	St Mary's Marsh, Blackmanstone, Newchurch, Kent	3U+EP	6./ZG 26
18 08 40	Bf 109 E-4	1990	Abbey Field, Leeds, near Maidstone, Kent	13+	2./JG 3
18 08 40	Ju 87 B-1	5167	Ham Manor Golf Course, Angmering, W Sussex	S2+JN	5./StG 77
21 08 40	Ju 88 A-1	-	Marsh Farm, Earnley, W Sussex	B3+BM	4./KG 54
24 08 40	Bf 109 E-4	5587	East Langdon, St. Margaret's at Cliffe, Kent	10+	6./JG 51
24 08 40	Bf 109 E-1	-	Minster Rd, Westgate, Kent	9+	1./JG 52
26 08 40	Do 17 Z-3	1207	Whepstead (Horringer), near Bury St Edmunds, Suffolk	U5+-	7./KG 2
26 08 40	He 111 P	-	Helliers Farm, Wick, near Littlehampton, W Sussex	G1+BB	Stab I./KG 55
26 08 40	He 111 P	2124	East Wittering Beach, Bracklesham Bay, W Sussex	G1+DM	4./KG 55
26 08 40	He 111 P	2165	West Brook Farm, Waterlooville, Hants.	G1+GM	4./KG 55
30 08 40	He 111 H	3305	Haxted Farm, Lingfield, East Grinstead, Surrey	V4+HV	5./KG 1
30 08 40	He 111 H	2782	Goodman's Farm, near Manston aerodrome, Kent	A1+JP	6./KG 53
30 08 40	Bf 109 E-1	3771	Westwood Court, near Faversham, Kent	12+	3./JG 27
31 08 40	Do 17 Z-3	2669	Sandwich Flats, near Princess Golf Club, Kent	5K+LM	4./KG 3
31 08 40	Bf 109 E-4	1082	Shoeburyness Beach, Kent	4+	3./JG 3
31 08 40	Bf 109 E-4	1184	Jubilee Hall Farm, Ulcombe, Kent	10+I	9./JG 26
31 08 40	Bf 109 E-7	5600	Chathill Park Farm, Crowhurst, south of Godstone, Surrey	13+	3./LG 2
01 09 40	Bf 109 E-4	1277	Haberdashers Wood, near Hamstreet, Ashford, Kent	14+	5./JG 54
01 09 40	Bf 110 C-1	985	Tarpot Farm, Tarpot Lane, Bilsington, Kent	L1+OH	13(Z)./LG 1
02 09 40	Bf 109 E-4	1261	Tile Lodge Farm, Hoath, near Westbere, Kent	12+	1./JG 52
03 09 40	Bf 110 C-4	3120	Edwins Hall, Stowmaries, Woodham Ferrers, Essex	3M+CB	Stab I./ZG 2
03 09 40	Bf 110 C-4	3113	Pudsey Hall Farm, Canewdon, near Rayleigh, Essex	3M+EL	3./ZG 2

Date	Aircraft	*Werknummer*	Location	Aircraft Code	Unit
04 09 40	Bf 110 C-1	2837	Church Farm, Washington, near Pulborough, W Sussex	2N+DP	Stab III./ZG 76
04 09 40	Bf 110 C-4	3545	English Channel off the Sussex coast	2N+AC	7./ZG 76
04 09 40	Bf 110 C-4	2116	Erringham Farm, Mill Hill, Shoreham-by-Sea, W Sussex	3M+AA	Stab/ZG 2
04 09 40	Bf 110 C-4	3101	Black Patch Hill, Patching, near Angmering, W Sussex	2N+CN	8./ZG 76
05 09 40	Bf 111 H-3	3324	Wantisden, Rendlesham, near Eyke, Suffolk	V4+AB	Stab I./KG 1
05 09 40	Bf 109 E-4	1985	Handen Farm, Claphill, Aldington, near Bilsington, Kent	6+	1./JG 3
05 09 40	Bf 109 E-4	1480	Loves Farm, Winchet Hill, near Marden, Staplehurst, Kent	<-+-	Stab II./JG 3
05 09 40	Bf 109 E-4	1096	6 Hardy Street, Maidstone, Kent	6+	Stab I./JG 54
06 09 40	Bf 109 E-7	5567	Hawkinge aerodrome, Kent	▲+C	6./LG 2
06 09 40	Bf 109 E-4	1506	Vincents Farm, North Manston, Kent	5+I	7./JG 53
07 09 40	Ju 88 A		Hafotty-y-Bulch, Mallwyd, Machynlleth, Wales	4U+BL	3(F)./123
07 09 40	Bf 109 E	5798	Wickhambreux, 5 miles east of Canterbury, Kent	11+	1./LG 2
09 09 40	Bf 109 E-1	6316	Coopers Field, Rosemary Farm, Flimwell, E Sussex	6+I	7./JG 3
09 09 40	Bf 109 E-4	1394	Knowle Farm, Mayfield, E Sussex	<+	Stab I./JG 27
09 09 40	Bf 109 E-1	3488	Charity Farm, Cootham, near Storrington, W Sussex	13+ -	5./JG 27
09 09 40	Ju 88 A	333	Beach, Pagham Harbour, W Sussex	4D+AD	Stab III./KG 30
09 09 40	Ju 88 A-1	274	Church Field, Newells Farm, Nuthurst, W Sussex	4D+AA	Stab/KG 30
11 09 40	He 111 H-3	5680	Burmarsh, near Dymchurch, Kent	1H+CB	1./KG 26
11 09 40	Bf 110 C-3	1372	Chobham Farm, Charing, near Ashford, Kent	U8+HL	2./ZG 26
15 09 40	Do 17 Z	2555	Lullingstone Castle Farm, Shoreham, Sevenoaks, Kent	F1+FS	8./KG 76
15 09 40	Bf 109 E-7	2058	Shellness, Isle of Sheppey, Kent	2+	3./LG 2
17 09 40	Bf 109 E-1	6294	Broomhill Farm, Camber, near Rye, E Sussex	2+I	7./JG 26
18 09 40	Bf 109 E-1	2674	Royal St Georges' Golf Links, Willow Farm, Sandwich, Kent	1+	9./JG 27
19 09 40	Ju 88 A-1	2151	Culford School, Bury St Edmunds, Suffolk	3Z+GH	1./KG 77
19 09 40	Ju 88 A-1	362	RAF Oakington aerodrome, Cambridgeshire.	7A+FM	4(F)./121
25 09 40	He 111 H	6305	Westfield Farm (Ballard Down), Studland, Dorset	G1+BH	1./KG 55

Date	Aircraft	Werknummer	Location	Aircraft Code	Unit
27 09 40	Bf 110 C-2	3560	Simmons Field, Mill Rd, Hailsham, E Sussex	L1+XB	Stab V./LG 1
27 09 40	Bf 110 C-4	3290	Kimmeridge, near Wareham, Dorset	3U+DS	8./ZG 26
27 09 40	Ju 88 A-1	8099	Graveney Marshes, near Faversham, Kent	3Z+EL	3./KG 77
30 09 40	Bf 109 E-4	1325	The Crumbles, near Langney, Eastbourne, E Sussex	13+-	3./JG 53
30 09 40	Bf 109 E-1	5175	Broomhill, near Strood, Rochester, Kent	12+I	7./JG 53
30 09 40	Ju 88 A-1	2142	Gatwick Race Course, Surrey	3Z+DK	2./KG 77
30 09 40	Bf 109 E-1	4851	Near Queen Anne's Gate, Windsor Great Park, Berkshire	9+	7./JG 27
30 09 40	Bf 109 E-4	1190	Alongside road at Eastdean, near Eastbourne, E Sussex	4+-	4./JG 26
02 10 40	Bf 109 E-4	5901	Addlested Farm, East Peckham, Paddock Wood, Kent	7+I	8./JG 53
03 10 40	Ju 88 A-1	4136	Eastend Green Farm, north of Hertingfordbury, Hertfordshire	3Z+BB	Stab I./KG 77
07 10 40	Bf 109 E-1	3881	Cross in Hand, Mayfield Flats, Hadlow Down, E Sussex	14+	5./JG 27
08 10 40	Bf 109 E-1	3465	Little Grange Farm, Hazleigh, Woodham Mortimer, Essex	2+	4./JG 52
12 10 40	Bf 109 E-4	4869	Near Chapel Holding, Small Hythe, Tenterden, Kent	<I+	II./JG 54
13 10 40	Bf 109 E-4	860	Cuckold Coombe, Hastingleigh, near Ashford, Kent	7+I	7./JG 3
17 10 40	Bf 109 E-7	4138	English Channel	8+	Stab I./JG 53
25 10 40	Bf 109 E-4	1988	Scotney Court Farm, Broom Hill, near Lydd, Kent	7+	5./JG 54
25 10 40	Bf 109 E-4	5104	Harveys Cross Farm, Telscombe, E Sussex	13+	3./JG 77
25 10 40	Bf 109 E-4	5178	West of Galloways Rd, Dungeness, E Sussex	2+	5./JG 54
27 10 40	Bf 109 E-4	3525	Penshurst Emergency Landing Ground, Kent	4+	3./JG 52
27 10 40	Bf 109 E-1	3576	Beach, near Lydd Water Tower, Kent	13+	7./JG 54
27 10 40	Ju 88 A-5	6129	Richmond Farm, Duggleby, Malton, near York	5J+ER	7./KG 4
29 10 40	Bf 109 E-4	5153	West Court Farm, near Wootton Crossroads, Shepherdswell, Kent	5+I	9./JG 3

Chapter 1

July

8 July 1940 at 1545 hrs

Messerschmitt Bf 109 E-3 (WNr. 1162), coded 4+, of 4./JG 51

Came down on Blabdean Hill, Elham, Kent.

Pilot: Lt Johann Böhm, who was captured.

The Bf 109 was attacked and damaged by Sgt E A Mould in a Spitfire of 74 Sqn (Hornchurch). Notably, it was the first German fighter shot down over the UK. Apparently, it took off from Desvres, near Boulogne. While in a formation of four aircraft, flying in line astern chasing a Spitfire, this aircraft was caught from below by another Spitfire which shot into the engine. The pilot put the aircraft into a dive to escape but was hit in the non-self-sealing fuel tank and crash landed with the undercarriage retracted.

Markings: white '4'.

11 July 1940 at 1210 hrs

Messerschmitt Bf 110 C-4 (WNr. 3551), coded 2N+EP, of 9./ZG 76.

Forced landing at Grange Heath, near Lulworth, Dorset.

Pilot: Olt Kadow.

The *Staffel* was ordered to protect Stukas that had targets in the Portland area. This Bf 110 was shot down by Green Section of 238 Sqn based at Middle Wallop (Fg Off Derek C MacCaw, Plt Off Harold J Mann and Sgt Cecil Parkinson). It was also harried by Sqn Ldr John S Dewar of 87 Sqn and Fg Off Christopher J H Riddle of 601 Squadron. It was the first Messerschmitt Bf 110 to be captured intact during the Battle of Britain.

According to Chris Goss (2000, p29), Kadow recalled:

We opened the fuel tanks and with the muzzle flash of my pistol I tried to inflame the gas of the fuel. I used up to 8 shots but had no success. Would I have had success I think the aircraft would have been exploded and we would be dead. I heard impacts around us, probably coming from bullets. I went around the aircraft in order to find out where the impacts were coming from. Doing so I got a blow into my heel. The bullet entered the rubber heel just when I made a step and due to the rubber of the heel the bullet was turned aside and left the heel on the left side of my boot so that my foot was hurt only by a flesh wound.

After this event we both left the aircraft alone and looked around. Then about 20 soldiers of the Coastguard stood up and an officer came nearer ordering hands-up, which we did, and took us prisoners of war. I told him that it was unfair to shoot at fliers being shot down. He said that we tried to destroy our aircraft and he tried to prevent this, 'Be glad' he said, 'that you haven't got shot in the belly'.

12 July 1940 at 1630 hrs

Heinkel He 111 P, coded G1+FA, of 5./KG 55

Crash landed opposite the Horse and Jockey Inn, Hipley, north-west of Portsmouth, Hampshire.

Pilot: Fw John Christian Möhn, who was captured unwounded. This pilot was wearing the Bronze Wound Badge which he was awarded for an action with ten Moranes in April 1940; this was the first time that someone wearing the badge had been captured.

The aeroplane started from west of Versailles flying alone on an armed reconnaissance flight. A photograph showing oil tanks was found, so presumably this was the objective. Coming in over the Isle of Wight and Southampton water it was attacked by fighters and promptly dropped its bomb load of sixteen 50kg bombs before crash landing opposite the Horse and Jockey Inn in Hipley. The aircraft remained relatively intact.

The aircraft was attacked by six Hurricanes from 43 Squadron (Tangmere), which were flown by Sqn Ldr J V C Badger, Flt Lt T F Dalton-Morgan, Plt Off R A De Mancha, Plt Off D G Gorrie, Plt Off H C Upton (Canadian) and Sgt C A H Ayling.

21 July 1940 at 1025 hrs

Messerschmitt Bf 110 C (WNr. 2177), coded 5F+CM, of 4(F)./14.

Came down at Goodwood Home Farm, Chichester, Sussex.

Crew: Olt Friedrich-Karl Runde (Ff) and Fw Willi Baden (Bf).

The Bf 110 took off from Cherbourg on a photographic reconnaissance mission over the centre of Southern England. It was fitted out for reconnaissance and had a camera in place of the two forward-firing cannons. While flying at 2,000ft, the aircraft was attacked by a Hurricane, which took out both of its engines.

24 July 1940 at 1300 hrs

Messerschmitt Bf 109 E-1 (WNr. 6296), coded <I+I, of Stab III./JG 26.

Landed on North Down, Broadstairs, next to Margate railway line, Kent.

Pilot: Lt Werner Bartels, who was severely wounded, was the technical officer of the *Gruppe*. He had spent five years in Brazil training and reorganizing the Brazilian Army under the French Mission. He was married to a Brazilian.

Lt Bartels started from St Inglebert, Calais. While on patrol, the whole *Gruppe* of some 40 aircraft was told by wireless that 40 or 50 109s were fighting over Dover and went to reinforce them. Before he got there, he was shot down by a Spitfire, which caught him beautifully with a deflection shot. He made a good forced landing and the aircraft was barely damaged. The aircraft was quite new, having only flown for ten hours.

Markings: black '<I+I', outlined in white.

Camouflage: air force blue throughout with blackened streaks on leading edges.

Armament: four machine guns were fitted. A new type of armour was fitted forming a back shield and a hood behind and above the pilot's seat.

28 July 1940 at 0500 hrs

Junkers Ju 88 A-1 (WNr. 7036), coded 9K+HL, of 3./KG 51.

Belly landed at Buckholt Farm, Sidley, Bexhill, East Sussex.

The mission started from Melun at 2230 hrs with four 250kg bombs, and the target was Crewe. The crew got completely lost following problems with the direction finder, and had almost reached Dublin when they realised that there was no blackout. They then headed west and then south, reaching London which they were convinced was Paris, whereupon they turned south again to find Melun but, presuming they had overshot, took the reciprocal course back over London. They then turned south once more and while over the Channel the pilot realised their mistake. With very little fuel left they jettisoned their bomb load, turned back and made a good forced landing.

Markings: yellow spinners.

Shield: a white edelweiss on a blue background.

The underside of the fuselage and wings were painted black.

The aircraft was delivered in January 1940.

After transportation, this aircraft was reassembled and shown at RAE Farnborough.

Chapter 2

August

8 August 1940 at 1515 hrs

Junkers Ju 87B-1, coded S2+LM, of 4./StG 77

Controlled force-landed west of St Lawrence, near Ventnor, Isle of Wight.

The aircraft sortied from Bougy, 15km south of Caen. While flying at 7,500ft on a mission to attack a convoy in the Channel, the engine failed. At 1,800ft it was attacked by fighters, the rear gunner was killed and the petrol lines were shot through. The dive-bomber was reported hit by Hurricane Mk I (SO-K) flown by Plt Off Peter L Parrott of 145 Sqn (Westhampnett).

11 August 1940 at 1040 hrs

Junkers Ju 88A, coded B3+DC, of Stab II./KG 54.

Force-landed at Blacknor Fort, Portland, Dorset.

Crew: Olt Karl Wette (Ff), Ofw Karl Meier (Bo), Gefr Walter Gehre (Bf) and Flgr Gottfried Kagenbauer (Bm). All the crew were captured.

The mission was a sortie to bomb Portland Harbour. The aircraft was damaged by an RAF Hurricane of 213 Sqn and was a write-off.

12 August 1940 at 1230 hrs

Messerschmitt Bf 110C-2, coded 2N+AN, of 8./ZG 76.

Shot down in combat with fighters and crashed in the sea off Portland.

Crew: Hptm Max Graf Hoyos (Ff), *Staffelkapitän*, and Uffz Siegfried Krommes (Bs). Both the pilot and gunner were listed missing in action.

Hoyos' personal account of the fighting in Spain, *Pedros Y Pablos*, (from which the photo of Hoyos is taken) was published by Verlag F Bruckmann in 1939 and copies can still be found through specialist booksellers.

12 August 1940 at 1215 hrs

Junkers Ju 88 A-1 (WNr. 3134), coded 9K+EL, of 3./KG 51

Exploded over Thorney Island. The main wreckage fell at Horse Pasture Farm, Westbourne, near Emsworth, West Sussex.

The Ju 88 started from Melun, south of Paris, at 1230 hrs. It was intercepted by fighters at 9,000ft, the wireless operator being killed and an engine hit. The aircraft went into a spin and the crew baled out. The aircraft broke up in the air, the rear gun position landing outside the Operations Room at Thorney Island aerodrome.

Markings: yellow 'E'; dark green upper surfaces and grey under wing.

Shield: a white starfish in the centre of a blue background; a yellow patch in the centre of the starfish.

12 August 1940 at 1300 hrs

Messerschmitt Bf 109 E-1 (WNr. 3367), coded 14+, of 2./JG 52

Good wheels-up landing close to Berwick rail crossing, Mays Farm, Selmeston, east of Lewes, Sussex.

Pilot: Uffz Leo Zaunbrecher, who was wounded.

The aircraft was severely damaged in an attack by Plt Off J A P MaClintock of 615 Sqn (Kenley) during combat over the coast near Hastings.

Markings: red '14'.

12 August 1940 at 1800 hrs

Messerschmitt Bf 109 E-1, coded <-+, of III./JG 54.

Force-landed at Hengrove, near Margate.

Pilot: Olt Albrecht Dress, who stated:

> I had luck that my aircraft did not catch fire, just that my engine and propeller reduction gear were hit, so I was forced to crash-land. I had suffered shrapnel wounds and was taken to Margate General Hospital and eventually to a prisoner-of-war camp at Grizedale Hall in the Lake District.

The Bf 109 is believed to have been attacked over the sea north of Dover and severely damaged by Spitfires from RAF Kenley during an escort sortie at 1750 hrs. The victory is believed to have been credited to Sgt Jack 'Jackie' Mann of 64 Sqn (Kenley) who was flying a Spitfire Mk I (SH-D).

The aircraft is shown at Hengrove, near Margate, Kent, being loaded on a trailer by men of 49 Maintenance Unit before being transported to RAF Faygate and then displayed around the UK (see below).

Markings: white '<-'.

13 August 1940 at 0645 hrs

Dornier Do 17 Z, coded U5+ER, of 7./KG 2.

Belly landed at Stodmarsh, near Canterbury, Kent.

The reconnaissance mission started from an aerodrome 15km south of Arras at 0400 hrs, and the aircraft was flying in a formation of two *Ketten* at a height of 600ft when attacked by fighters from Red and Blue sections of 111 Sqn Hurricanes (Croydon). The attackers put one engine out of action and with the petrol and oil leads shot through the pilot belly landed the aircraft.

Markings: white 'E'.

Shield: the top half showed a red cross on a white background and the lower half had a white cross on a red background.

The emblem of KG 3 was carried by this unusually marked Dornier of 7./KG 2. It had probably just been transferred between the units. Although not immediately apparent, the aircraft does have the KG 2 nose-stripe which can be seen emerging from behind the shield in the photo. Note that it is flaking off above the shield.

Armament: five machine guns were carried. This aircraft was more heavily armoured than any other that had been examined previously.

ADLER TAG/EAGLE DAY
13 August 1940 at 0710 hrs

Messerschmitt Bf 109 E-1 (WNr. 5068), coded <+, of I./JG 2 Richthofen.

Pilot: Olt Paul Temme, *Gruppe Adjutant*.

The Bf 109 took off from Beaumont Le Roger on a fighter sweep operation. Having problems with his engine, it got left behind by the rest of the formation and, while going to the assistance of a straggling Junkers Ju 88 bomber, was shot down by 43 Sqn Hurricanes from Tangmere. Sgt J P Mills ultimately adding this victory to his tally.

The aircraft belly landed on New Salts Farm, Shoreham-by-Sea, West Sussex, in a cornfield to the south of Shoreham aerodrome, between the main coast road and the coastal railway. The hangars and control tower/terminal building, which are all still fully operational to this day, can be seen in the background of the photograph (see above).

13 August 1940 at 0725 hrs

Dornier Do 17 Z, coded U5+DS, of 8./KG 2.

Shot down onto the mudflats at Seasalter, Kent, where it smashed to pieces.

Crew: three of the four crew were killed. The fourth crew member, Fw Rudolf Hänsten (Bm), was badly wounded.

Took off from Doai at 0700 hrs with the rest of the *Staffel*, later being joined by aircraft from I and II./KG 2, forming a formation of about 40 aircraft. The mission was to bomb Eastchurch aerodrome. This aircraft was attacked by Hurricane fighters from 111 Sqn (Croydon) and 151 Sqn (North Weald) at 6,000ft. It was a combined attack and the aircraft was shot down by Flt Lt H M Ferris (111 Sqn) and Sgt J T Craig (151 Sqn).

13 August 1940 at 0830 hrs
Dornier Do 17 Z, coded U5+KA, of Stab/KG 2.

Crashed on the railway, Pherbec Bridge, Barham, Kent.

Pilot: Olt Heinz Schlegel.

The aircraft started out from St Leger, near Arras, at 06.30 hrs to bomb Eastchurch aerodrome, with ten 50kg bombs. An RAF intelligence report states: 'Flying westwards over the Thames Estuary, [the aircraft] was attacked by a Spitfire that came out of the sun and put shots into the tail and motor.'
   It is believed that it was engaged by attacking fighters from both 111 Sqn (Croydon) and 74 Sqn (Hornchurch) over north Kent and was probably the one claimed by Plt Off J A Walker of 111 Sqn,

flying a Hurricane. The aircraft was wrecked whilst forced landing into a railway cutting. Remarkably, the pilot and all the crew survived.

Markings: green 'K'.

Shield: a bomb falling from a cloud with a man sitting on it holding a telescope.

13 August 1940 at 1635 hrs
Junkers Ju 88 A-1, coded L1+BS, of 8./LG 1

Crashed at Great Ham Farm, Earnley, near Selsey, West Sussex, and exploded on impact, killing all on board.

Pilot: Major Alfons Scheuplein.

The target for the Ju 88 was RAF Middle Wallop. It was attacked by 257 Sqn Hurricanes from Northolt flown by Sgt A G Girdwood and Fg Off L R G Mitchell of 'A Flight'.

15 August 1940 at 1700 hrs

Messerschmitt Bf 110 C, coded 2N+BC, of Stab III./ZG 76.

Ditched in the sea at Weymouth Bay, Dorset.

Crew: Hptm K F Dickoré (Ff) (see left), *Gruppenkommandeur*, whose body washed ashore at Le Touquet, France; and Uffz H Templin (Bf), who baled out.

The Bf 110 was on escort duties. Another Bf 110, flying higher, was shot down and in falling hit this aircraft, which was also brought down.

Markings: green 'B'; two-tone green upper surfaces; first version of the *Wespe* (bees on a cloud) emblem on the nose. The emblem, three small wasps above clouds, was designed by Lt Richard Marchfelder (see photograph on page 52).

15 August 1940 at 1830 hrs

Junkers Ju 88 A, coded L1+ SM, of 4./LG 1.

Crashed and burnt out at Priors Leaze, Breach, Woodmanscote, Westbourne, Sussex.

Pilot: Ofw Willi Richter, who was wounded.

Crew: Olt Möller, who was the unit's technical officer; Gefr Erhard Anders (Bs) and Olt Harald Möller (Bo), who both died; and Fw Heinz Dittmann (Bm), who was wounded.

A trophy from the aircraft is displayed by 601 Sqn based at RAF Tangmere (see above left).

15 August 1940 at 1830 hrs
Junkers Ju 88 A, coded L1+FM, of 4./LG 1.

Great Ham Farm, Earnley, near Selsey, West Sussex.

Crew: Uffz W Rimek, who died, Uffz F Dieter, Gefr W Hohbom and Uffz Otto Rezeppa (Bf/Bs) (see right).

The Ju 88 took off from Orléans for a bombing sortie against RAF aerodromes in the Portsmouth area, including Tangmere and Westhampnett. It was shot down by Flt Lt S D P Connors in a Hurricane of 111 Sqn (Croydon).

15 August 1940 at 1830 hrs

Messerschmitt Bf 110 C-6, coded S9+TH, of 1./ErpGr 210.

Ended up as a pile of smashed wreckage at Broadbridge Farm, Smallfield, near Horley, Surrey.

Crew: Lt Erich Beudel (Ff) (see below left) and Ogefr Otto Jordan (Bf) (see below right).

The Bf 110 was shot down on return from a mass attack on Croydon aerodrome and was armed for ground attacks as it was fitted with one large gun, an MK 101 30mm Rheinmetall machine gun, instead of two 20mm cannon. Eight magazines of ten rounds each were also discovered. The crew baled out too low and perished.

15 August 1940 at 1850 hrs

Messerschmitt Bf 110 D (WNr. 3339), coded S9+CB, of ErpGr 210.

Landed at School Farm, Hooe, East Sussex.

Crew: Lt Karl-Heinz Koch (Ff) and Uffz R Kahl (Bf).

ErpGr 210 was again in action on 15 August, in an attack against the RAF fighter airfield at Kenley in Surrey. However, the raiding force mistook RAF Croydon, a few miles to the north, as being RAF Kenley. A devastating attack against Croydon was carried out but it was not without cost to the attacking force. Among them was this aircraft, flown by *Gruppe* technical officer Lt Karl-Heinz Koch, which was shot down by fighter action as it headed towards the Sussex coast on its way home.

   The radio operator/gunner, Uffz Rolf Kahl, was hit by multiple machine-gun bullets which left him very badly wounded. As a direct consequence, he was repatriated to Germany via the Red Cross in 1943.

THE CROYDON RAID (BLACK THURSDAY)
15 August 1940 at 1900 hrs
Messerschmitt Bf 110 D (WNr. 3338), coded S9+AB, of ErpGr 210.

Came down at Bletchlinglye Farm, Catts Hill, Rotherfield, East Sussex.

Crew: Hptm Walter Rubensdörffer (Ff) (see left) and Ogefr Ludwig Kretzer (Bf) (see far left).

ErpGr 210 carried out its deepest penetration raid to date. However, the attack did not go well. Firstly, the fighter escort from JG 52 'lost' their assigned bomber formation on the way to the target. Then the aircraft, which were approaching from the east, directly into the evening sun, making identification of the target in the haze almost impossible, bombed Croydon airfield rather than the briefed target of Kenley.

Croydon airfield received a warning that an attack was imminent and 111 Sqn scrambled at 1905 hrs, a few minutes before it was bombed. Yellow Section met the Bf 110s head-on at the bottom of their dive. Blue 1, B Flight Sqn Ldr Thompson was at the centre of this action and reports suggest he inflicted damage on S9+AB in particular.

Following the attack, defensive circles were formed south of Croydon before the Bf 110s fled on their return towards the Channel. The raid was then successfully intercepted near Redhill by 32 Sqn (Biggin Hill) a few minutes later. Also in the vicinity were 501 Sqn (Gravesend) who were put up to cover the Gravesend to Gatwick areas. Blue 2 Pilot Officer Duckenfield is credited with teaming up with 32 Sqn who subsequently confirmed his part in this notable victory. Although great damage had been caused at Croydon, the attacking aircraft, 14 Bf 110s and eight Bf 109s, suffered very heavy losses.

15 August 1940 at 1910 hrs
Messerschmitt Bf 110D-0/B (WNr. 3341), coded S9+CK, of 2./ErpGr 210.

Force-landed at Hawkhurst, Kent.

Crew: Olt Alfred Habisch (Ff) and Uffz Ernst Elfner (Bf). Both survived and were taken into captivity.

The aircraft had left Denain aerodrome, Nord-Pas-de-Calais, France, on a bombing mission over Southern England. After the attack, it was intercepted by Hurricanes of 32 Sqn and 111 Sqn. With the wireless operator wounded and the undercarriage damaged, the pilot managed to make a forced landing at Hawkhurst in Kent.

The aircraft is shown on public display in the second half of August 1940 at Garnault Place, Finsbury, North London (see above left). It was also exhibited at Hendon to raise money for the Spitfire Fund. In April 1941, the whole aircraft was shipped to Los Angeles aboard the SS *Montanan*, where it was reassembled and evaluated by the Vultee Aircraft Company.

15 August 1940 at 1910 hrs

Messerschmitt Bf 109 E-4/B (WNr. 1910), coded 3+, of ErpGr 210.

Came down at Lightlands, Frant, East Sussex.

Pilot: Horst Marx.

Marx was flying his Bf 109 as a fighter escort. After the attack on Croydon he had seen a damaged Bf 110 heading away and he attempted to protect it from further attacks. The pilot had radioed that he was wounded and his gunner was already dead.

The pilot was none other than his commanding officer, Walter Rubensdörfer. Marx turned to head off an attack, but bullets from a Hurricane's guns damaged his engine and Marx was forced to take to his parachute over Frant near Tunbridge Wells, Sussex.

Markings: yellow '3'.

16 August 1940 at 1300 hrs

Junkers Ju 87 B-2 (WNr. 5580), coded T6+HL, of 3./StG 2.

Skidded across the B2145, Selsey Road, near Church Norton Junction, Sussex.

The Ju 87 was engaged by Hurricanes of 43 Sqn from Tangmere during a direct attack on their base, as well as by Spitfires from nearby 602 Sqn (Westhampnett). It was finally shot down by Sqn Ldr J V C Badger of 43 Sqn. The aircraft was in good condition but less its undercarriage, with radiator damage, which caused engine failure. The two crew were discovered by Air Intelligence personnel badly wounded in a hospital near Chichester and would not give any details.

16 August 1940 at 1300 hrs

Junkers Ju 87 B-1 (WNr. 5618), coded T6+KL, of 3./StG 2.

Crash landed at Bowley Farm, South Mundham, West Sussex.

Crew: Fw Heinz Rocktäschel (Ff) and Ofw Willi Witt. Both died of their wounds during the engagement.

Flt Lt Boyd of 602 Sqn (Westhampnett) reported that he'd only just left the ground when he saw a Ju 87 pulling out of its dive right in front of him and he immediately opened fire with a two-second burst (600 rounds) at about 600ft. Boyd completed his circuit and landed again without raising his wheels! Both Flt Lt Boyd and Flt Lt Davis of 601 Sqn (Tangmere) describe their Stuka as crash landing through trees and bushes with both wing tips being ripped off. The plane was found to be riddled with 240 rounds.

16 August 1940 at 1705 hrs

Heinkel He 111 P (WNr. 1582), coded G1+FR, of 7./KG 55.

Belly landed (shot to pieces) on Honeysuckle Lane, High Salvington, Worthing, West Sussex.

Crew: Lt Rudolf Theobald (Ff) (see bottom left), who was captured and taken prisoner of war, and Uffz Weber (Bm) (see bottom right), who was killed.

The He 111 P was on a bombing sortie to attack Great West aerodrome (Heathrow Airport). On the return leg of the sortie, it was intercepted at 1655 hrs at 2,500ft over Brighton by three Spitfire MK1s flown by 602 Squadron, City of Glasgow, Blue Section, which were based at RAF Westhampnett, near Chichester.

Flight Lieutenant Robert Findlay Boyd, Spitfire (N3227) gave the following report:

Sighted Enemy Aircraft approx. 1,000ft above and coming towards us. Blue 1 did climbing turn and delivered beam attack, followed by Blue 2 who stopped one motor. Successive attacks were delivered by Section until enemy aircraft crashed on waste ground approx. 4 miles north of Worthing.

Just over a couple of weeks later, on 4 September, another enemy aircraft fell just a stone's throw away in the next field. As it was just off the Honeysuckle bridleway there was easy access and the wreckage attracted quite a gathering of the press and made front-page news.

16 August 1940 at 1730 hrs

Messerschmitt Bf 110 C-4 (WNr. 3278), coded 2N+CC, of Stab II./ZG 1.

Crashed at Droke, near Upwaltham, East Dean, West Sussex.

Crew: Marchfelder (Ff) (see far left) and Jentzsch (see left), who both survived, parachuting to safety near Amberley; the pilot wrenched his knee badly on landing.

On the return leg of their escort sortie for the Heinkels of KG 55, Kaldrack, the formation leader, detached Marchfelder from the *Stabschwarm* and ordered him to hang behind, at safe altitude, to keep an eye out for crippled bombers. He was to radio the *Gruppe* for help in the event of any trouble. Their aircraft crashed 6 miles away at Droke, near Upwaltham, north of Chichester. Victory was claimed by the Spitfire of Sqn Ldr Sandy Johnstone of 602 Sqn based at Westhampnett.

2N+CC is seen with its distinct green 'C' at the firing butts – presumably in France in early summer 1940 (see left).

Note: the mission on 16 August 1940 was the last sortie over England before II./ZG 1 was reorganised as III./ZG 76. However, it would appear that the re-designation of some Messerschmitt Bf 110 units took place at the end of June 1940 (i.e. II./ZG 1 became III./ZG 76 and I./ZG 52 became II./ZG 2).

16 August 1940 at 1815 hrs

Heinkel He 111 P (WNr. 2217), coded G1+HP, of 6./KG 55.

Landed alongside Bostal-Sompting track, close to Hill Barn, Steyning, West Sussex.

Crew: Olt Wilhelm Wieland (Ff), Fw Langstrof (Bo), Uffz Appell (Bf), Uffz Hattendorf (Bm) and Uffz Pulver (Bs). Hattendorf and Pulver were both killed.

The aircraft took off from Chartres carrying sixteen 50kg bombs to be used to attack aerodromes. It was shot down by fighter action, which led to a fractured oil system and engine failure, which was followed by a good belly landing.

Markings: yellow H and spinners.

Shield: a red griffon.

A 615 Squadron RAF Intelligence Report stated:

Pilot Officer Lofts – Blue 3

Broke away from his Section and attacked a Heinkel 111 which was straggling behind from astern, he gave it one long burst closing to 150 yards, the enemy aircraft dived through the clouds.

Blue 3 followed it down, which glided down and made a landing near Steyning. The aircraft appeared to be intact.

Before Blue 3 flew away he noticed soldiers surrounding the Heinkel.

This was subsequently confirmed by the Army.

18 August 1940 at 1320 hrs

Dornier Do 17 Z-2 (WNr. 334), coded F1+HT, of 9./KG 76.

Crashed at 'Sunnycroft', Golf Road, Kenley, Surrey.

Pilot: Olt Hans-Siegfried Ahrends.

The Dornier was hit by groundfire and PAC (parachute and cable) defences during a low-level attack on Kenley and crashed and burned out north of the airfield at 1320 hrs. Being a Sector Station, Kenley was a vital link to the inner ring of RAF aerodromes protecting the capital.

For the operation to knock it out, KG 76 employed all three *Gruppen* dispersed on three airfields around Paris. The first two waves of bombers were intercepted before they hit the airfield and instead of finishing off what was left, the 9th *Staffel* reached Kenley first.

Aboard one of the Dorniers, a Luftwaffe war correspondent, Rolf von Pebal, took a series of aerial pictures, including one taken over Cyprus Road, Burgess Hill, while they were outward bound (see below) and one taken directly over RAF Kenley where a blast pen containing a No. 64 Squadron Spitfire is quite clear (see below).

18 August 1940 at 1330 hrs

Dornier Do 17 Z-2, coded F1+DT, of 9./KG 76.

Came down at Leaves Green, near Biggin Hill, Kent.

The aircraft took off from an airfield near Paris with the whole *Staffel* for a low-level attack on Biggin Hill aerodrome, with the alternative target being Kenley aerodrome.

After releasing bombs on Kenley aerodrome the aircraft was hit by AA fire and crashed. The engines and cockpit were destroyed by fire and a large number of bullet holes were found in the main planes and tail assembly.

Just after mid-day the heaviest formations of enemy aircraft yet seen during the battle stimulated 11 Group to bring every serviceable aircraft it had to readiness. Two consecutive raids hit Biggin Hill before the sector station at Kenley came under heavy attack from coordinated waves at low and medium level.

Both formations were intercepted, but severe damage was caused with all ten hangars and 12 aircraft, including ten Hurricanes, being destroyed. The runways were heavily cratered, although still usable, and the communications network was so badly affected that the Sector Operations Room had to be moved to an emergency location off the airfield.

For the rest of the battle, Kenley could accommodate only two squadrons instead of three. At Croydon, one of the previously undamaged hangars was hit and West Malling was also bombed.

The photograph (see right) shows that missing swastika panel from the tail fin, which is on display at the RAF Museum Hendon.

18 August 1940 at 1335 hrs

Messerschmitt Bf 110 C (WNr. 3102), coded 3U+EP, of 6./ZG 26.

Landed at St. Mary's Marsh, Blackmanstone, Newchurch, Kent.

The Bf 110 was shot down by several fighters while on bomber escort duties but landed in excellent condition. It appeared to be a brand-new aircraft.

Markings: yellow 'E'.

Shield: a red diamond edged in white.

Camouflage: green all over.

18 August 1940 at 1350 hrs

Messerschmitt Bf 109E-1 (WNr. 1990), coded 13+, of 2./JG 3.

Wheels-up landing at Abbey Field, Leeds, near Maidstone, Kent.

Pilot: Olt Helmut Tiedmann, a *Staffelkapitan* of 2./JG 3. His squadron name was 'Udet'. He had seven victories to his credit.

At approximately 1300 hrs local time, Flight Sergeant Philip Tew, flying a Spitfire of 54 Sqn (RAF), was attacked by Olt Tiedmann at around 2,000ft. Tew turned towards Tiedmann in a diving turn, at which

point Tiedmann half rolled and followed his target down. Tew pulled out of the sweeping dive at low altitude, but Tiedmann was already in trouble. He was forced to make a successful wheels-up landing in open country at Leeds Castle, near Maidstone, and his propeller bent on impact. Villagers had noted the engine sounded like it was sputtering as it crashed, which turned out to be bullet strikes to the radiator.

Apparently, Tiedmann had quickly abandoned his crashed plane. Local Home Guard were first to the scene but were not quick enough to apprehend the plot and found the chute had also not been used. It took another 12 hours before he was captured. He'd been trying to make it to the coast to steal a small boat. He had survival on rations for two days and had a compass on him.

Markings: black '13'.

18 August 1940 at 1423 hrs

Ju 87 B-1 (WNr. 5167), coded S2+JN, of 5./StG 77.

Landed at Ham Manor Golf Course, Angmering, West Sussex.

Crew: Ofw K Schweinhardt and Ofw William Geiger.

The dive-bomber was involved with the precision attack on the British Fighter Command radar station at Poling in Sussex. As seen here, it is being guarded by local Home Guard at Ham Manor Golf Course. It landed on its wheels and was almost intact despite the thirty .303 holes plus anti-aircraft splinter marks all along the glass top and fuselage.

The losses of Junkers 87 Stuka dive-bombers during the day were so severe that, apart from a few later isolated sorties, this type of aircraft was withdrawn from the main battle by the Germans.

21 August at 1615 hrs

Junkers Ju 88 A-1, coded B3+BM, of 4./KG 54.

Came down at Marsh Farm, Earnley, West Sussex.

Crew: Ofw Heinz Apollony (Ff), Hptm Lothar Maiwald, Uffz Kurt Miethner and Uffz Helmut Hempel.

In the photograph below, the pilot follows the crew captain of this aircraft, Hptm Lothar Mainwald. This was notably a position often held by an officer (acting as observer) flying with an NCO pilot such as in this case.

24 August 1940 at 1255 hrs

Messerschmitt Bf 109 E-4 (WNr. 5587), coded 10+, of 6./JG 51.

Crash landed at East Langdon, near Dover, Kent.

Pilot: Ofw Fritz Beeck, who was taken prisoner of war.

The pilot was taking part in his second sortie of the day; the first starting at 1000 hrs escorting about 20 bombers, which were attacking an aerodrome near Canterbury. After a quick lunch he set off again with about seven aircraft from his *Staffel*, and some from 2./JG 51, to escort a further 20 bombers attacking an aerodrome near Margate. He engaged with a number of Hurricanes and Spitfires but believed he had received no hits. However, on the way home an oil pipe broke and, as the engine was failing, he made a forced belly landing. The Bf 109 was hit in the nose by 12 strikes from below.

Markings: yellow '10', wings and tail tips.

Shield: a weeping raven with spectacles and an umbrella. On the tail were three yellow stripes and above these were the dates 7/7/40, 29/7/40 and 15/8/40, signifying three successes and their dates.

24 August 1940 at 1545 hrs

Messerschmitt Bf 109 E-1, coded 9+, of 1./JG 52.

Came down near to Minster Road, Westgate, Kent.

Pilot: Fw Herbert Bischoff.

While on an aggressive patrol near London at 18,000ft, the pilot was surprised by fighters from behind and hit in the engine and radiator, so came in to land in a cornfield and took off one wing on an electric grid pylon.

Markings: white '9'.

Shield: a black boar on a white background.

26 August 1940 at approx. 1540hrs

Dornier 17 Z-3 (WNr. 1207), coded U5+-, of 7./KG 2.

Force-landed at Horringer, near Whepstead, Bury St Edmunds, Suffolk.

Crew: only the gunner, Gefr Ludwig Schadt, escaped injury. He was notably the youngest of the crew (second from left). He was soon escorted away into captivity by the military authorities to nearby RAF Stradishall.

The raiding formation was heavily mauled on the way in by nearby Hurricanes vectored from Duxford, Debden and North Weald, but a few reached their targets and dropped their bombs. This aircraft managed to reach RAF Debden to do just that and tried to make good a hasty escape but was spotted in between cloud, intercepted and engaged by three Hurricane fighters, led by Squadron Leader McNab of 1 Sqn (RCAF) (see above right), who pressed home their relentless attack. With three of his crew wounded, the pilot was driven to make a forced landing with one engine disabled from having a cylinder shot off.

On this occasion, the Luftwaffe received a different kind of warm welcome, this time a field of real mustard destined for Colman's of Norwich. With so much labour expected to be close by attending to the harvest, no doubt within just a few moments the crew could reliably expect a hostile welcome party armed with pitchforks!

26 August 1940 at 1630 hrs
Heinkel He 111 P, coded G1+BB, of Stab I./KG 55.

Force-landed at Helliers Farm, Wick, near Littlehampton, West Sussex.

Crew: Olt Ignaz Krenn (Ff) and Uffz Helmut Morrack (Bo), who were both taken prisoner; Uffz Hans Degen (Bf), Uffz Willi Schneiders (Bm), who was wounded; and Fw Alois Schreek (Bs), who was seriously wounded.

The flight path adopted for the mission was Rembouillet, Dreux, Portsmouth. Before reaching the objective of Portsmouth docks, this aircraft was attacked by six or seven fighters who shot at it, stopping first one and then the other engine. The bombs were scuttled shortly before the aircraft made a good forced landing.

Markings: white 'B' with a red stripe inside it.

Shield: a gold and red dragon with blue wings.

26 August 1940 at 1630 hrs
Heinkel He 111 P (WNr. 2124), coded G1+DM, of 4./KG 55.

Came down 50 yards out to sea at East Wittering beach, Bracklesham Bay, West Sussex.

The aircraft started from Chartres at 1542 hrs with the objective of bombing Portsmouth. It was attacked by fighters that damaged the port engine, causing it to catch fire, and broke the oil feed to the starboard engine. The pilot shut off both engines and made a forced landing on the beach at low tide. The crew were prevented from setting fire to the aircraft. Between 400 and 500 .303 strikes were generally distributed over the aircraft.

Markings: white 'D'.

Shield: a red and white dragon with blue wings on a gold background.

Armament: MG 15, one fixed gun, firing out of the extremity of the tail.

26 August 1940 at 1645 hrs
Heinkel He 111 P (WNr. 2165), coded
G1+GM, of 4./KG 55.

Crashed at West Brook Farm, Waterlooville,
Hampshire.

The bomber started from Chartres to bomb
Portsmouth Docks. Before reaching its
target, it was attacked by fighters which shot
up both engines. The starboard engine seized
due to oil radiator being shot through. Also
damaged by AA fire, the aircraft hit a tree on
crashing and broke in half.

Markings: white second 'G'.

30 August 1940 at 1135 hrs
Heinkel He 111 H (WNr. 3305), coded V4+HV, of 5./KG 1.

Force-landed at Haxted Farm, Lingfield, East Grinstead, Surrey.

Pilot: Fw Schnabel.

The Heinkel had already bombed Farnborough when it was intercepted by a Hurricane of 253 Sqn
flown by Pilot Officer Greenwood.
   The pilot made a good forced landing. Plt Off Greenwood reported that he followed the Heinkel
down, saw it make a belly landing and flew so low he could see the crew climb out. Two injured crew
were taken to hospital and the remaining three were held at a searchlight post at Chellows until they
were taken away for interrogation.
   Several .303 bullet strikes were found in the oil radiators, and oil can be seen to have been thrown
up around the engine and propeller. Later, this Heinkel was put on display to raise money for the local
Spitfire Fund.

30 August 1940 at 1715 hrs

Heinkel He 111 H-2 (WNr. 2782), coded A1+JP, of 6./KG 53.

Came down at Goodman's Farm, near Manston aerodrome, Kent.

Crew: Fw Karl Eckert (Ff) and Gefr Koehler (Bf), who both died; Gefr Klapp (Bo) and Gefr Gluck (Bs), who were wounded; Fw Stoeckl (Bm), who was taken prisoner of war.

The aircraft started out at about 1400 hrs from near Armentieres with the objective of bombing an aerodrome north of London. On preliminary interrogation, it was stated that the whole of *Gruppe* II was at the aerodrome near Armentieres and that 12 aircraft, with an escort of Bf 109s took part in this raid. It was intercepted at about 13,000ft by fighters, near the River Crouch, and when the pilot was badly wounded, the observer took control. Damage was also possibly caused by AA fire. The bomb load jettisoned over the Thames.

Markings: yellow 'J'; '2782' painted in black on the tail.

30 August 1940 at 1645 hrs
Messerschmitt Bf 109 E-1
(WNr. 3771), coded 12+, of
3./JG 27.

Landed at Westwood Court,
near Faversham, Kent.

Pilot: Fw Ernst Arnold.

The Bf 109 started on a
freelance patrol at 1600
hrs. It was surprised by an
attack by Spitfires which hit
the radiator and forced the
aircraft to land, which it did
in good condition. About
thirteen .303 strikes traced in
the aircraft.

Markings: yellow '12';
orange engine cowling.

Shield: tiger's head with a map
of Africa as the background.

31 August 1940 at 1420 hrs

Dornier Do 17 Z-3 (WNr. 2669), coded 5K+LM, of 4./KG 3.

Force-landed on the foreshore at Sandwich Flats, 200 yards from the Princess Golf Club, Sandwich, Kent.

About 15 aircraft of KG 3 started from Antwerp, at 1300 hrs with a fighter escort of Bf 109s to attack an aerodrome east of London, which they thought was Hornchurch. Having bombed their target, they were attacked by fighters and then they were fired at by a Vickers .303 gun which claims to have brought them down, although bullet strikes in the tail indicate fighter action. Once they had come down, the crew set light to the aircraft. The crew were caught and became prisoners of war (see below).

31 August 1940 at 1845 hrs

Messerschmitt Bf 109 E-4 (WNr. 1082), coded 4+, of 3./JG 3.

Beached at Shoeburyness, Kent.

Pilot: Olt Helmut Rau.

The Bf 109 started from France at 1630 hrs on a freelance patrol which consisted of two formations of eight aircraft. When flying at nearly 30,000ft it was attacked from the rear by a British aircraft. The pilot had tried to climb out of danger, which he thought was possible until he lost his wingman, who he saw had been hit, and in a steep, out-of-control dive, was then himself hit in the engine forcing him to come down on the beach at Shoeburyness. The aircraft was found to be in good condition.

Markings: yellow '4', with black edges; three stripes on the tail representing one Morane on 13/5/40 and two Curtis' on 14/5/40.

Shield: a dragon's head with a yellow snake-like body, outlined in black with a very protruding long red tongue.

Armament: four machine guns; one in each wing and two firing through the airscrew from the top of the engine.

The aircraft was constructed by Erla, Leipzig, with the *werknummer* 1082, dated 15/7/40.

31 August 1940 at 1845 hrs

Messerschmitt Bf 109 E-4 (WNr. 1184), coded 10+I, of 9./JG 26.

Force-landed during the early evening at Jubilee Hall Farm, Ulcombe, Kent.

Pilot: Olt Wilhelm Fronhöfer of Stab III./JG 26 was one of three pilots shot down. He can be seen 'off-duty' in the image on the right.

During a late-afternoon mission, the entire *Geschwader* took off to rendezvous with KG 76, which was to attack the RAF aerodrome at Hornchurch. As soon as the aircraft of III./JG 26 crossed the coast, they were attacked by RAF fighters. This aircraft was believed to have been shot down by Plt Off Colin Gray of 54 Squadron.

31 August 1940 at 1845hrs

Messerschmitt Bf 109 E-7 (WNr. 5600), coded 13+, of 3./LG 2

Came down at Chathill Park Farm, Crowhurst, south of Godstone, Surrey.

Pilot: Von Perthes.

Markings: brown '13'.

Chapter 3
September

01 September 1940 at 1115 hrs

Messerschmitt Bf 109 E-4 (WNr. 1277), coded 14+, of 5./JG 54.

Crashed at Haberdashers Wood/Burnt Oak Wood at Orlestone, near Hamstreet, Ashford, Kent.

Pilot: Olt Anton Stangl, *Staffelkapitän*.

The Bf 109 took off from an aerodrome in Belgium and while on escort duties towards the target, collided with another 109 from unit 1./JG 52, flown by Ofw Paul Gerber, who was killed. Stangl, however, successfully baled out.

Both machines came down in close proximity (Gerber between Orlestone Church and the main road and Stangl behind the church).

Markings: yellow aircraft nose.

Note: the Austrian emblem, the 'Lion of Aspern', was adopted towards the latter part of 1940.

01 September 1940 at 1400hrs
Messerschmitt Bf 110 C-1 (WNr. 985), coded L1+OH, of 13(Z)./LG 1.

Belly landed at Tarpot Farm, Tarpot Lane, Bilsington, Kent. Both engines of the aircraft were out.

Crew: Ofw Rudolf Kobert (Ff) (see below left, where he is shown at readiness) and Fw Werner Meinig (Bf).

In the photograph (see below right), a policeman and a soldier inspect the ruptured earth caused by a passing German bomber that was trying to destroy the aircraft to keep it out of enemy hands. The poles are the anti-glider posts that were erected in fields across southern England to discourage invasion landings.

2 September 1940 at 1740 hrs
Messerschmitt Bf 109 E-4 (WNr. 1261), coded 12+, of 1./JG 52.

Crashed at Tile Lodge Farm, Hoath, near Westbere, Canterbury, Kent.

Pilot: Fw Heinz Urlings, who was captured and taken away to be interrogated.

The Bf 109 started out at 1700 hrs on a freelance patrol with four other aircraft. It developed engine trouble and while it was making a forced landing it was attacked by a Hurricane. It crashed due to the engine being hit by .303 strikes and the port wing being torn off.

Markings: white '12', wing and tail tips; white upper and lower surfaces; white aft half of the rudder.

Shield: a black running boar on a white background.

Armament: two MG 17s and two 20mm cannons.

Armour: standard bulkhead but nothing protecting the pilot.

3 September 1940 at 1100 hrs
Messerschmitt Bf 110 C-4 (WNr. 3120), coded 3M+CB, of Stab I./ZG 2.

Crashed at Edwins Hall, Stowmaries, Woodham Ferrers, Essex.

While flying at 19,000ft on bomber escort duties, this aircraft was attacked by six Spitfires when the crew went to help another Bf 110 which was in trouble. Both crew baled out and the aircraft dived into the ground at high speed, both wings breaking off.

The rare original colour photograph (see below) of 3M+DB of ZG 2 was taken in France in early 1940. It clearly represents a good example of a *Gruppenstab* aircraft, thus providing a suitable impression for 3M+CB, which had a distinct 'green C' (rather than the 'green D' of 3M+DB) also applied on its outer wing surfaces. Note the distant line-up of Messerschmitts carry their position codes in white and, in comparison, have contrasting all-over camouflage of their own (see page 51, 3M+EL).

3 September 1940 at 1500 hrs

Messerschmitt Bf 110 C-4 (WNr. 3113), coded 3M+EL, of 3./ZG 2.

Crashed at Pudsey Hall Farm, Canewdon, near Rayleigh, Essex.

The Bf 110 flew across to England 'looking for trouble' and was engaged from above by three Spitfires. Both crew baled out and the aircraft dived into the ground and was buried at a depth of 20ft. The crew were taken prisoner of war.

4 September 1940 at 1320 hrs

Messerschmitt Bf 110 C-1 (WNr.2837), coded 2N+DP (formerly 2N+DC before unit re-designation, apparently in June 1940), of Stab III./ZG 76.

Hit the ground and exploded at Church Farm, Washington, near Pulborough, West Sussex.

The aircraft dived in flames from great height into a field and was totally destroyed. It was not possible to obtain any information as the aircraft was lying in a 20ft-deep crater. Smoke and flames from the burning wreck also gave up the position of No. 461 Battery, Royal Artillery, during the raid.

In the space of barely 30 minutes on this fateful day, no fewer than six Bf 110s crashed on the South Downs between Shoreham-by-Sea and further westwards, just off the coast, at Littlehampton, West Sussex.

Markings: three wasps on a cloud, painted on the nose.

4 September 1940 at 1340 hrs

Messerschmitt Bf 110 C-4 (WNr. 3545), coded 2N+AC, of 7./ZG 76.

Lost over the Channel off the Sussex coast.

Crew: Ofw Konrad Daum (Ff) and Uffz Ferdinand Mayer (Bf).

Markings: two-tone green upper surfaces typify an early *Wespe*, complete with the nose art designed by Lt Richard Marchfelder. Most notably, the three wasps on a cloud emblem was adopted and carried by III./ZG 76 around this time.

4 September 1940 at 1350 hrs

Messerschmitt Bf 110 C-4 (WNr. 2116), coded 3M+AA, of Stab/ZG 2.

Force-landed at Erringham Farm, Mill Hill, Shoreham-by-Sea, West Sussex.

The Bf 110 took off at 1235 hrs. It was attacked by five Spitfires and the port engine stopped. As the situation was getting desperate, the crew made a good forced landing.

Badge: a horizontal red lightning flash.

Engine: DB601. A number of .303 strikes in each engine indicated that both engines had cut out.

4 September 1940 at 1345 hrs

Messerschmitt Bf 110 C-4 (WNr. 3101), coded 2N+CN, of 8./ZG 76.

Force-landed at Black Patch Hill, Patching, 4 miles north-east of Angmering, West Sussex.

While on escort duties, before reaching its objective, this aircraft was attacked by a Spitfire from below and was not seen by the crew. The right engine caught fire and the pilot made a forced landing.

With the intention of destroying all equipment, the crew shot flare cartridges into the cockpit. The aircraft caught fire two minutes later and was burnt out.

Markings: black 'C', outlined in white; red spinners.

Badge: three wasps on the fuselage.

5 September 1940 at approx. 0110 hrs

Heinkel He 111 H-3 (WNr. 3324), coded V4+AB, of Stab I./KG 1.

Crashed at Wantisden, Rendlesham, near Eyke, Suffolk.

Pilot: Hans-Dietrich Biebrach.

Originally targeted to bomb Tilbury Docks, the pilot turned northwards and snaked downwards, trying to avoid the lights. However, he could not escape. A Blenheim on night patrol from Martlesham Heath got on his tail and stopped the port engine, the bomb load being ditched. He then partly escaped the searchlights but was very quickly picked up again and flying at 1,000ft, with half the crew wounded, they decided to bale out. The pilot actually jumped and made a good landing from 650ft.

The destruction of two night raiders by the same RAF night-fighter crew (Plt Off M J Herrick and Sgt J S Pugh) without AI (radar) in one night was an extraordinary achievement at this time in 1940.

Of the five crew seen in the line-up (see below), only the pilot, Hans-Dietrich Biebrach, (centre) survived. The body of one missing crewman was not found until October 1942 when a tree knocked down by a bomb revealed his remains hidden in the upper branches.

As seen here, the beer flowed and soon 25 Squadron (Blenheims) trophy cabinet contained some newly acquired prized possessions (see bottom right). It is believed the MG 15-wielding RAF officer (see top right)

is none other than the victorious pilot, Mike Herrick. The beer bottles and his improperly dressed appearance tell their own story.

One such machine gun saved from this aircraft is on display at the Kent Battle of Britain Museum Trust.

THIS MG 15 HAND HELD MACHINE GUN WAS RECOVERED FROM A JUNKERS JU 88, AT A DEPTH OF APPROXIMATELY 100'T, OFF THE FAIRLIGHT CLIFFS, EAST SUSSEX. NOTHING CERTAIN IS KNOWN OF ITS HISTORY.

A GERMAN SADDLE DRUM MAGAZINE, AS USED WITH THE MG 15 HAND HELD MACHINE GUN. THIS HAD A CAPACITY OF 75nn x 7 ROUNDS. THIS EXAMPLE IS FROM A HEIN 111, THE HISTORY OF WHICH IS UNKNOWN

AT 3.10AM ON THURSDAY 5TH SEPTEMBER 1940 A HEINKEL HE 111H-3 (3324) OF STAB 1/KG1 WAS SHOT DOWN BY A BLENHEIM NIGHT-FIGHTER FLOWN BY P/O M. J. HERRICK AND SGT. J. S. PUGH OF NO. 25 SQUADRON. IT WAS ON A BOMBING SORTIE OVER TILBURY WHEN IT WAS CAUGHT IN SEARCHLIGHTS AND THE PORT ENGINE DISABLED. THE CREW DUMPED THEIR BOMBS AND BALED OUT AT LOW LEVEL. MAJOR L. MAIER (GRUPPENKOMMANDEUR), OBERFW. E. STOCKERT AND UFFZ. H. BENDIG WERE KILLED. OBERLT. J-W. GRAF VON RITTBERG BALED BUT WAS KILLED. OBERLT. H. D. BIERBACH BALED OUT AND WAS CAPTURED UNHURT. THE AIRCRAFT CRASHED AT THE VILLAGE OF BUTLEY, A FEW MILES FROM WOODBRIDGE, SUFFOLK.

THIS MG 15 HAND HELD MACHINE GUN WAS TAKEN AT THE TIME AND LATER DONATED TO THE MUSEUM. TO THE RIGHT IS A PICTURE OF THE HEINKEL HE 111, TAKEN SHORTLY AFTER THE CRASH. IT IS BELIEVED THAT THE GENTLEMAN HOLDING THE MG 15 MACHINE GUN IS P/O MICHAEL J. HERRICK. MR. B. R. BUFF, WHOSE AUNT OWNED THE FIELD IN WHICH THE HEINKEL CRASHED, KINDLY DONATED THIS PICTURE.

PILOT OFFICER MICHAEL JAMES HERRICK

5 September 1940 at 1010 hrs

Messerschmitt Bf 109 E-4 (WNr. 1985), coded 6+, of 1./JG 3.

Force-landed at Handen Farm, Claphill, Aldington, near Bilsington, Kent.

Pilot: Lt Heinz Schnabel, who was slightly wounded.

The Bf 109 started at 0840 hrs, escorting Dorniers that were attacking Croydon. On return from the attack some Spitfires and a Hurricane split this aircraft off from the formation and shot into its engine. The pilot made a good forced landing, but the engine mounting broke off at the bulkhead. About fifteen .303 strikes were spread over the fuselage.

Markings: white '6', outlined in black; white rudder and wing tips; two vertical stripes on the rudder (victory tabs).

Shield: a white worm, outlined in black with a red tongue.

5 September 1940 at 1010 hrs
Messerschmitt Bf 109 E-4 (WNr. 1480), coded <-+-, of Stab II./JG 3.

Wheels-up landing at Winchet Hill, Loves Farm, Marden, Staplehurst, Kent.

Pilot: Franz von Werra, who was featured in the book and film, *The one That Got Away*. An account of his story is below:

Firstly recaptured whilst making escape from Grizedale Hall, he was transferred to another camp converted out of a conference centre at Hayes, near Swanwick in Derbyshire. This was the scene of his second attempted escape which led to what the RAF called the 'Hucknall Incident'. His ingenious plan was to pose as a Dutch Allied pilot, infiltrate an aerodrome and steal an aircraft to fly back to occupied France.

Helped by other prisoners, he worked out a clever cover story whereby he would claim to have been shot down while returning to a remote base near Aberdeen after a bombing raid on Denmark.

Another prisoner had retained his flying suit which, along with a good pair of boots, helped provide a disguise to make this story appear more convincing. They also knew that they were between Sheffield and Nottingham and that Hucknall lay not far to the south.

The 'shot-down Dutch pilot' fiction was quite convincing to civilians, including the Stationmaster at Codnor Park who was harassed and busy issuing tickets to factory worker commuters arriving early the next morning. The problem with the story, of course, was where are the rest of the crew? And why didn't we notice your Wellington coming down? It was good enough, however, for the Great Northern Railway men and even for the C.I.D., some of whom the Stationmaster wisely called before notifying the RAF.

The bluffing German airman was slightly worried when he learned that most of the RAF pilots at Hucknall were Poles, though he managed to avoid meeting any of them. The British officers he did encounter were not particularly convinced by the 'Dutch pilot' and deliberately kept him near a roaring fire to try to get him to remove his (suspicious, non-regulation) flying overalls. They also wanted to see the forged dog-tag – which he realized had melted into a sticky blob!

While the British Duty Officer was trying to telephone the 'Dutchman's' Scottish base, von Werra slipped out and made a run towards Hurricanes he had previously observed parked nearby.

What he did not realise was that although half the base was run by the RAF, the other half [was operated] by Rolls-Royce. After being very lucky so far about avoiding armed guards for the top-secret site he strode up to one of the Hurricanes and coolly ordered a nearby mechanic to prepare it for take-off. He also requested some cockpit instruction since he was unfamiliar with the type. Before the 'trolley-acc.' could be brought over the Duty Officer re-appeared with his pistol...

5 September 1940 at 1115 hrs

Messerschmitt Bf 109 E-4 (WNr. 1096), coded 6+, of Stab I./JG 54.

Dived out of control and crashed into 6 Hardy Street, Maidstone, Kent.

Pilot: Uffz Fritz Hotzelmann.

This aircraft became engaged in a dog fight over Biggin Hill and the engine was damaged. The pilot tried to escape and was followed for some distance by a Spitfire; the engine eventually failed when it was near Maidstone. The pilot baled out, as the plane was a complete wreck.

Markings: white top of the rudder and tail planes.

Shield: a chimney sweep carrying a ladder; this emblem was only used by aircraft of I./JG 54

6 September 1940 at 1814 hrs
Messerschmitt Bf 109 E-7 (WNr. 5567), coded ▲+C, of 6./LG 2.

Emergency landed at Hawkinge aerodrome, Kent.

Pilot: Fw Werner Gottschalk, who was wounded.

The aircraft started its bomber-escort mission at 1730 hrs from a small aerodrome approximately 40 miles south-east of Boulogne. It flew from Cap Gris Nez to the Thames Estuary at a height of 12,000ft and was hit by AA fire near Chatham. The petrol tank was hit and the pilot turned for home but ran out of petrol and landed at Hawkinge. The engine cooling system showed a number of .303 strikes.

Markings: yellow '+C'; black triangle outlined in white; white rudder and wing tips, the white having been painted on yellow; blue and white spinner with black vertical stripes.

Camouflage: two shades of grey on the upper surfaces and standard duck-egg blue on the lower surfaces.

Armament: two MG 17s over the engine, two 20mm cannons in the wings.

There was an external faired-in bomb rack which appeared to be for carrying 50 kg bombs. In the cockpit there was a selector panel and also a bomb jettisoning handle. A button on the joy stick was probably a bomb-release button.

6 September 1940 at 1850 hrs

Messerschmitt Bf 109 E-4 (WNr. 1506), coded 5+I, of 7./JG 53.

Wheels-up landing at Vincents Farm, North Manston, Kent.

Pilot: Uffz Hans Georg Schulte.

The aircraft started out at 1730 hrs on a freelance patrol. It was flying with four others from the same *Staffel* at a height of 16,500ft when it was shot down by fighters. The pilot tried to land at Manston aerodrome.

Markings: white '5', 'I', spinner, cowling and rudder; painted-out thick red band round the cowling.

Camouflage: mottled light and dark green and grey.

One wing was buckled but otherwise the aircraft was in a fair condition.

7 September 1940 at 1230 hrs

Junkers Ju 88 A, coded 4U+BL, of 3(F)./123.

Crashed into a mountainside in low cloud at Hafotty-y-Bulch, Mallwyd, Machynlleth, Montgomeryshire, Wales.

The crew had been carrying out daily photo-reconnaissance over Liverpool for some time. However, this time they were chased from their objective by Spitfires and one engine was hit.

7 September 1940 at 1735 hrs

Messerschmitt Bf 109 E (WNr.5798), coded 11+, of 1./LG 2.

Landed at Wickhambreux, approx. 5 miles east of Canterbury, Kent.

Pilot: Uffz Werner Götting. He refused to talk in a preliminary interrogation.

The aircraft was attacked by Spitfires and the pilot baled out. The Bf 109 was smashed to pieces and buried in a crater. 'White 11' is shown as it appeared in France earlier in 1940 (see below).

9 September 1940 at 1800 hrs
Messerschmitt Bf 109 E-1 (WNr. 6316), coded 6+l, of 7./JG 3.

Landed at Coopers Field, Rosemary Farm, Flimwell, Sussex.

Pilot: Uffz Matthias Massmann.

The Bf 109 started at 1715 hrs on a freelance patrol, which consisted of one *Staffel*, along the coast. While flying at 25,000ft, when over the coast, they were surprised by a Spitfire coming out of the sun which shot this aircraft from behind through the engine. It landed with its undercarriage retracted and was in good condition.

Markings: white '6' and '1' with black edges; yellow spinner and rudder.

Armament: four MG 17s.

Armour: standard bulkhead and armoured shield behind the pilot's head.

Fuel: 87 octane.

The aircraft constructed by Gerhardt Fieseler, Cassel.

This aircraft was fitted with dive and horizontal bomb gear between the pilot's knees, apparently for four bombs, size unknown. A technical note stated: 'Red line on glass indicated a dive angle of about 45°. Usual landing flaps were used to limit speed in dive-bombing, having lines to show 0°, 10°, 20°, 30°, 40°; the 40° line being marked in red.' This confirmed that the German fighter was on a bombing mission.

Some of the salvaged Bf 109 fighters were kept in a hangar at RAE Farnborough in 1940 (see above and right). All aspects of Luftwaffe aero engineering were studied with interest.

After close inspection and examination, component designs were evaluated as to their potential development capability in the arms race for ultimate superiority.

9 September 1940 at 1745 hrs

Messerschmitt Bf 109 E-4 (WNr. 1394), coded <+, of Stab I./JG 27.

Force-landed at Knowle Farm, Mayfield, East Sussex.

Pilot: Oberleutnant Gunther Bode, *Gruppe Adjutant.*

The aircraft's radiator had been hit and damaged during a mission to escort bombers to London. While flying at about 16,000ft, two Spitfires suddenly appeared above and this aircraft was shot through the radiator with the first burst. Turning for home, the engine began to overheat and the aircraft landed in good condition, except for damaged undercarriage. At the time of combat the formation was fairly near London but could not see it because of a slight mist.

The aircraft was initially covered in camouflage netting by the military prior to removal to Stanhay's Garage, Ashford, for exhibition and later to Barretts Garage, Canterbury. This aircraft was put on public display at different venues around the UK to raise money for the Spitfire Fund. It is shown being exhibited at Stanhay's Garage in Ashford, Kent.

9 September 1940 at 1750 hrs

Messerschmitt Bf 109 E-1 (WNr. 3488), coded 13+-, of 5./JG 27.

Force-landed on Charity Farm, Cootham, near Storrington, West Sussex.

Pilot: Olt Erwin Daig.

Started from Calais, escorting bombers to London. Following attack by a fighter at 20,000ft, from below and astern, the radiator and petrol tank were hit and the pilot force-landed. The aircraft was recovered in a good condition.

Markings: long red dash with white edging; black '13' with a white border; yellow cowling and rudder.

The aircraft is shown on display in Dudley in the West Midlands (see above).

9 September 1940 at 1750 hrs

Junkers Ju 88 A (WNr. 333), coded 4D+AD, of Stab Ill./KG 30.

Force-landed on the beach, Pagham Harbour, West Sussex.

Pilot: Major Hackbarth, *Gruppekommandeur*, who was the son-in-law of Generalfeldmarschall Albert Kesselring, who was the senior commanding officer of Luftflotte 2.

Crew: Ofw Manger, Uffz Sawallisch and Gefr Petermann. Two of the crew did not survive, including Petermann.

The aircraft was participating in a raid on the London Docklands area during the late afternoon. It was attacked by fighters, who hit the starboard engine and holed both radiators. As both engines were finally disabled, the propellers feathered, and with all the crew already either dead or wounded, the pilot had no choice but to make a forced landing on the foreshore at Pagham Harbour, West Sussex.

This aircraft was on the way out of London when it was believed to have been attacked by Spitfires of 602 Squadron, Sqn Ldr A V R Johnstone, Plt Off A Lyall and Fg Off P C Webb.

9 September 1940 at 1800 hrs

Junkers Ju 88 A-5 (WNr. 274), coded 4D+AA, of Stab/KG 30.

Landed at Church Field, Newells Farm, Nuthurst near Horsham, West Sussex.

Crew: Olt Rolf Heim (Ff), Uffz Josef Beck, Fw A Fuhs and Uffz Walter Baustian. All were taken prisoner of war.

The Ju 88 took off 1530 hrs with four 250kg bombs. Its target was the London docks, the same mission having been carried out successfully the previous day. However, before reaching the objective the formation was attacked by 12 Spitfires. The Perspex roof, together with machine guns, was jettisoned, the oil radiators were hit and the pilot made a belly landing.

11 September 1940 at 1600 hrs

Heinkel He 111 H-3 (WNr. 5680), coded 1H+CB, of 1./KG 26.

Force-landed at Burmarsh, near Dymchurch, Kent.

Pilot: Hans Friedrich.

The aircraft started from Courtrai at 1440 hrs on a mission it bomb the London docks. The formation was met by the escort at Dover and some time later, when near London, this aircraft was hit by AA fire, which was followed by an attack by fighters. The bombs were jettisoned near Sevenoaks, Kent, and the aircraft made a forced landing. The aircraft was set on fire by the crew and completely destroyed.

11 September 1940 at 1700 hrs

Messerschmitt Bf 110 C-3 (WNr. 1372), coded U8+HL, of 2./ZG 26.

Landed at Chobham Farm, Charing, near Ashford, Kent.

Crew: Fw Hermann Brinkmann (Ff) (see right) and Uffz Erwin Gruschow (Bf).

The Bf 110 started out from St. Omer at 1600 hrs with between 20 and 30 fighters forming the escort for Heinkel 111s. Before reaching the objective, while flying at 13,000ft, an engine defect developed and while coming down this aircraft was attacked by a Spitfire. It landed with a retracted undercarriage. A number of .303 strikes were traced from an astern attack.

Markings: yellow 'H'; white nose; white band round the fuselage, forward of tail plane; white rings on the spinners; the crest, an old-fashioned railway engine in white, was painted out with white.

BATTLE OF BRITAIN DAY
Sunday 15 September 1940 at 1210 hrs

Dornier Do 17 Z (WNr. 2555), coded F1+FS, of 8./KG 76.

Landed at Lullingstone Castle Farm, Shoreham, Sevenoaks, Kent.

Crew: Fw R Heitsch (Ff), who was captured unhurt; Fw S Schmid, who was captured severely wounded but died later that day; Fw H Pfeiffer and Fw M Sauer, who were captured wounded.

The aircraft started out from Beauvais at 1045 hrs to attack the Thames docks, crossing the coast at about 15,000ft near Dover, with 11 other bombers. By noon that day about 100 German bombers were flying in a 10-mile front over north Kent, heading for London. Flying to intercept them, were nine RAF Squadrons. Flight Lieutenant John C Dundas and Pilot Officer Eugene 'Red' Tobin of 609 Squadron pursued a Dornier 17Z of 8./KG 76 down the Darent Valley, Kent.

Three of the German crew were wounded in the air and the bombs were dropped live into a field. The aircraft landed with a retracted undercarriage; the starboard engine had stopped before landing. The starboard and port airscrews were pierced with .303 strikes.

The Army, at the time was stationed at Lullingstone Castle, put a guard on the aircraft before it was taken away.

15 September 1940 at 1445 hrs

Messerschmitt Bf 109 E-7 (WNr. 2058), coded 2+, of 3./LG 2.

Force-landed at Shellness, Isle of Sheppey, Kent.

Pilot: Klick.

This Bf 109 was attacked by Spitfires and hit in the radiator. It was forced to land badly.

Markings: brown '2'.

17 September 1940 at 1730 hrs

Messerschmitt Bf 109 E-1 (WNr. 6294), coded 2+I, of 7./JG 26.

Wheels-up landing at Broomhill Farm, Camber, near Rye, East Sussex.

Pilot: Uffz Karl Heinz Bock.

The Bf 109 started out from an aerodrome 3km from Guines at 1630 hrs on a freelance patrol with the whole of the JG 26 *Geschwader*.

When nearing London, the engine began to fail and the pilot turned for home but had to make a forced landing. The wings were buckled and broken but the fuselage and engine were in a fair condition.

Markings: white '2' and 'I', outlined in black; yellow nose.

Armament: four MG 17s.

Armour: there was no head shield for the pilot.

18 September 1940 at 1310 hrs

Messerschmitt Bf 109 E-1 (WNr. 2674), coded 1+, of 9./JG 27.

Came down on Royal St Georges' Golf Links, Willow Farm, Sandwich, Kent.

Pilot: Gefr Walter Glöckner, who was wounded.

The *Staffel* moved to Calais on 14 June 1940, having previously been at Cherbourg. On this operation eight aircraft set out in formation – two Vic 3s and a *Rotte*. The pilot of this aircraft was in the 2nd Vic and was not told what the mission was, just to follow the leader. Over Canterbury they were attacked by Spitfires and the petrol pipe of this aircraft was hit. The pilot force-landed and set fire to the aircraft after a good belly landing.

Markings: yellow rudder and nose; figure '1' on the cowling; three concentric yellow rings on the spinner.

The remains of Glöckner's Bf 109 is shown being transported past the Houses of Parliament (see above).

19 September 1940 at 1130 hrs

Junkers Ju 88 A-1 (WNr. 2151), coded 3Z+GH, of 1./KG 77.

Came down at Culford School, Bury St Edmunds, Suffolk.

Crew: Uffz Ernst Etzold (Ff), who was wounded, was the only survivor from the four-man crew.

The aircraft was initially heading across north Kent towards the Thames estuary area. The target was believed to be London but before it could reach it, the aircraft was intercepted and pursued by Hurricane fighters of 249 Squadron (North Weald) and 302 Squadron from Duxford and was eventually shot down in flames, becoming a burnt-out wreck in the grounds of Culford School. In the combat report it describes the incident taking place over Mildenhall, Suffolk, and timed at 1130 hrs as submitted by Plt Off Julian Kowalski from 'B Flight', 302 Sqn.

19 September 1940 at 1500 hrs

Junkers Ju 88 A-1 (WNr. 362), coded 7A+FM, of 4(F)./121.

Belly landed at RAF Oakington aerodrome, Cambridgeshire.

Pilot: Uffz Hans Jurgen Scheket.

The Ju 88 started out from Caen at 1400 hrs on a photographic and weather reconnaissance mission. On the return journey, having taken photographs, the port engine developed a defect and as the crew saw a number of fighters coming up, they made a forced landing with the undercarriage retracted. The crew stated that they belly landed because the aerodrome was so small and that the Ju 88 was difficult to handle on just one engine.

   A few .303 bullet holes were recorded in the port engine and cockpit. The observer had already taken out the film from the camera and fogged it. All four crew members were captured uninjured and the aircraft was later dismantled and dispatched to RAE Farnborough for examination.

25 September 1940 at 1200 hrs

Heinkel He 111 H (WNr. 6305), coded G1+BH, of 1./KG 55.

Crashed on Westfield Farm, Studland, near Swanage, Dorset.

Pilot: Fw Fritz Jürgens.

The aircraft started out from Dreux at 1100 hrs with the objective of attacking the Bristol Aero Engine works. The flight took place between 9,000ft and 15,000ft. After bombing the target, this aircraft was surprised from the rear by three Spitfires, two of which attacked from above and one from below. The starboard engine was hit and bursts of .303 are traced halfway down the fuselage and in the wings. The pilot was wounded and made a forced landing with the undercarriage retracted.

Markings: white 'B'.

Camouflage: dark green all over with lamp black on the under surfaces and covering white spinners.

27 September 1940 at 0950 hrs

Messerschmitt Bf 110 C-2 (WNr. 3560), coded L1+XB, of Stab V./LG 1.

The wreckage was spread across Simmons Field, Mill Road, near Hamlins Mill, Hailsham, East Sussex.

Pilot: Hptm Horst Liensberger (see below right).

Flight Lieutenant Burton (see below left) led 249 Squadron in a diving attack out of the sun. The Bf 110 collided with a British fighter and its tail was cut off. The aircraft crashed with the crew inside and was completely destroyed.

27 September 1940 at 1200 hrs

Messerschmitt Bf 110 C-4 (WNr. 3290), coded 3U+DS, of 8./ZG 26.

Belly landed 0.75 miles west of Kimmeridge, near Wareham, Dorset.

Crew: Uffz Fritz Schupp (Ff) and Gefr Karl Nechwatal (Bf), who were both wounded.

The aircraft started from Cherbourg at 1100 hrs escorting bombers to the Bristol Aero Engine works. When the formation arrived just east of Portland, on the way to the objective, it was attacked by Spitfires. This Bf 110 was flying at 21,000ft when it was attacked by two Spitfires coming out of the sun, one attacking from each side. The port engine caught fire and the pilot force-landed. The starboard engine was shot through in the fuel system and both rudders and wings showed many .303 strikes. Despite this, the aircraft was in a fairly good condition.

Markings: 'D' – a very thin black line outlined with a broad white line; yellow squares on the two rudders and tail plane; dark green spinners with a red ring; two yellow bars and three white stripes with roundels against them with the dates, '10/07/40' and '18/07/40' (twice).

The usual 87 octane number for the fuel carried had been painted over with a yellow triangle and C.2 painted on the triangle in black. A yellow triangle was painted over all the petrol filling caps.

27 September 1940 at 1530 hrs

Junkers Ju 88 A-1 (WNr. 8099), coded 3Z+EL, of 3./KG 77.

Force-landed at Graveney Marshes, 4 miles north-east of Faversham, Kent.

Crew: Uffz Frita Ruhlandt (Ff) (see right) and Uffz Erwin Richter (Bf), who were wounded; Uffz Gotthardt Richter (Bo); and Gefr Jakob Reiner (Bs), who was also wounded. This was his first war flight, having only been with the unit for seven days.

The flight path adopted for the mission was to fly north-west from Laon to landfall between Dover and Folkestone, heading for the Thames Estuary north of Gillingham. This aircraft was damaged by AA and then attacked by Spitfires, which damaged the engines. The pilot made a forced landing and the crew, who at that time were unwounded, tried to set fire to their aircraft and fired at it with a Tommy Gun. The crew are also said to have fired at people trying to prevent them from destroying their aircraft and coming to arrest them. During the subsequent engagement three of the crew were wounded.

30 September 1940 at 1405 hrs
Messerschmitt Bf 109 E-4 (WNr. 1325), coded 13+-, of 3./JG 53.

Belly landed at the Crumbles, near Langney, Eastbourne, East Sussex.

Pilot: Fw Walter Scholz.

The Bf 109 started out from Etaples at 1430 hrs escorting bombers, the fighters joining with the bombers when near the English coast, with the fighters flying at 19,000ft. The pilot claimed there was no combat but he made a forced landing because he was short of petrol. However, a few .303 strikes were traced in the cooling system and engine.

Markings: yellow '13' and horizontal bar; orange nose, rudder and fin.

Armament: two 20mm cannons and two MG 17s.

Armour: standard cross bulkhead and panel behind the pilot's hood.

30 September 1940 at 1410 hrs
Messerschmitt Bf 109 E-1 (WNr. 5175), coded 12+I, of 7./JG 53.

Crash landed at Broomhill, near Strood, Rochester, Kent.

Pilot: Uffz Ernst Poschenrieder, who was wounded.

The Bf 109 started out at 1300 hrs on escort duties with the whole *Gruppe*. Before reaching the objective, this aircraft, which was flying at 19,000ft on the extreme right of the escort formation, was attacked from above by several Spitfires. The radiator and engine were hit and the pilot made a crash landing.

Markings: white '12' and 'I'; yellow nose and rudder.

Camouflage: blue and green dappled yellow and green on the upper surface, sky blue beneath.

30 September 1940 at 1645 hrs
Junkers Ju 88 A-1 (WNr. 2142), coded 3Z+DK, of 2./KG 77.

Came down at Gatwick Race Course, Surrey.

Pilot: Olt Friedrich Oeser.

The aircraft started out from Laon on a mission to bomb London. Before reaching the objective, it was hit by AA fire and the pilot being wounded by shrapnel, decided to return. It was then attacked by fighters and one of the engines was hit in the first attack. The aircraft tried to escape into clouds but they were attacked a second time and the other engine was hit, forcing them to land. On inspection, forty .303 strikes were found to be generally distributed over the aircraft with a few traced in the cooling system.

Markings: black 'D', outlined in white; red spinners.

Crest: a black eagle with a yellow flag and the words, 'Ich das will dass si vorvechten'.

3Z+DK was put on public display at Primrose Hill, north London.

30 September 1940 at 1700 hrs

Messerschmitt Bf 109 E-1 (WNr. 4851), coded 9+, of 7./JG 27.

Belly landed near Queen Anne's Gate, Windsor Great Park, Berkshire.

Pilot: Olt Karl Fischer.

The mission was to act as a bomber escort. When the formation was on its way to the objective it was attacked by fighters. Soon after the dogfight broke off, the pilot assumed he had no significant damage. However, a radio transmission from his pair told him that he had a white petrol plume streaming behind and looking at his petrol gauge he noticed that the tanks were almost empty, so he made a forced landing but overturned. There were a number of bullet strikes from astern.

Markings: white '9' painted on a yellow engine cowling; white spinner with a black circle on the tip. (Old factory markings had been painted out viz. PH+LV.)

As was typical at the time, Fischer's Bf 109 was taken around the country for public display.

Markings: white '9'.

30 September 1940 at 1730 hrs

Messerschmitt Bf 109 E-4 (WNr. 1190), coded 4+-, of 4./JG 26.

Landed alongside main coast road at Eastdean, near Eastbourne, East Sussex.

Pilot: Uffz Horst Perez, who was wounded.

The Bf 109 started out from an aerodrome between Boulogne and Etaples at about 1600 hrs on bomber escort duties. The aircraft flew inland at 16,000ft westward towards Eastbourne and then inland towards London. It was supposed to be escorting bombers but never located them, so circled to the north of Eastbourne. It was then intercepted at 28,000ft and made for the coast. However, the engine failed, presumably shot by ground defences (a few strikes hit at an angle of 45° through the cooling system) so the pilot force-landed the aircraft.

On getting out of his aircraft, the pilot was shot at and wounded in the hand and jaw.

Markings: previously had been '<+'; yellow nose and fin.

Crest: a tiger's head in natural colours on the port side of the fuselage.

Shield: white with a black 'S'.

There was a 100 octane triangle mark on the fuselage.

The photograph (see right) gives a rare close-up view of 1190's tail fin illustrating detailed victory tabs.

W.Nr. 1190

Chapter 4
October

2 October 1940 at 1015 hrs
Messerschmitt Bf 109 E-4 (WNr. 5901), coded 7+I, of 8./JG 53.

Landed on Addlested Farm, East Peckham, south-west of West Malling Aerodrome, Kent.

Pilot: Olt Walter Fiel, who survived. It is noted that 26-year-old Fiel had already been awarded the Iron Cross First Class and had previously served with JG 3.

The aircraft started out from Boulogne. When flying at 16,000ft, it was attacked by about 16 Spitfires and hit in the radiator. The pilot dived away to the left and tried to get home by flying in a cloud layer at 5,000ft. Eventually, the engine seized up and Fiel crash landed with his engine backfiring near Peckham, Kent. Although there were very few .303 strikes in this machine, Fiel's radiator, petrol tank and probably the fuel lines were hit.

Markings: black '7' and 'I', outlined in white; yellow nose with a wide red band; red spinner.

The aircraft was fitted with bomb gear.

3 October 1940 at 1140 hrs

Junkers Ju 88 A-1 (WNr. 4136), coded 3Z+BB, of Stab I./KG 77.

Crashed at Eastend Green Farm, 1 mile north of Hertingfordbury, Hertfordshire.

Pilot: Olt Biegward Siebig. The crew were all captured.

The Ju 88 started out from between Laon and St. Quentin at 1030 hrs to bomb Reading aerodrome. The course was from near Laon, over Dieppe, towards Reading, making landfall at Worthing. As the crew could not locate their main target, owing to bad visibility, they flew around the countryside looking around for another target. They sighted and bombed the De Havilland's works that adjoined Hatfield aerodrome and came down to 100ft before releasing the bombs. However, they were attacked by ground defences at the aerodrome and were hit by MG fire and Bofors gunfire. Both engines were damaged and caught fire causing the aircraft to come down in flames. The crew jumped out without their parachutes, apparently before the aircraft actually touched down.

Markings: yellow 'K' and a white patch on the upper surface of the port wing; yellow 'B' on the starboard wing with no white patch; this Ju 88 wore the white tactical stripe on the port side only.

Crest: a black eagle on a yellow shield inside a grey shield, outlined in black.

7 October 1940 at 1645 hrs

Messerschmitt Bf 109 E-1 (WNr. 3881), coded 14+-, of 5./JG 27.

The wreckage fell at Cross in Hand, Mayfield Flats, Hadlow Down, near Heathfield, Sussex.

Pilot: Uffz Paul Lege, who was a veteran of some 48 operational flights over England.

The Bf 109 started from Bonningues, near Calais. It was attacked by a Hurricane and came down in flames. It was completely destroyed and the pilot was unable to escape from his aircraft.

Uffz Paul Lege can be seen casually posing with his regular mount on an airfield in France (see left). Subsequently, the same aeroplane would carry him to his death whilst engaging enemy fighters.

8 October 1940 at 0925 hrs

Messerschmitt Bf 109 E-1 (WNr. 3465), coded 2+, of 4./JG 52.

Came down at Little Grange Farm, Hazleigh, Essex.

Pilot: Fw Paul Boche, who was captured wounded.

Pilot Officer Ronald 'Ras' Berry of 603 Squadron flying a Spitfire Mk I XT-N claimed this as a probably destroyed as he hit the fighter in the radiator over the Thames Estuary, 2 miles south of RAF Hornchurch. The engine overheated and stopped.

Markings: white '2'.

Note the on-lookers just above the hedge line in the left photograph.

12 October 1940 at 1020 hrs

Messerschmitt Bf 109 E-4 (WNr. 4869), coded <I+, of 4./JG 54.

Belly landed at Chapel Holding, Small Hythe, Tenterden, Kent.

Pilot: Lt Bernhardt Malischewski.

The pilot made a very good belly landing. Malischewski claimed that the engine just gave out and he had not been shot down. There were no signs of .303 strikes or AA fire and the engine did not appear to have overheated.

   Local soldiers make quick use of camouflage netting and an abundance of fresh hay from the recent harvest to hide from opportunist aerial sabotage.

   The aircraft was later erected for display at Lincoln and demonstrated that unusual style of *Stab* markings typical of JG 54 (see below).

13 October 1940 at 1410 hrs

Messerschmitt Bf 109 E-4 (WNr. 860), coded 7+I, of 7./JG 3.

Crashed at Cuckold Coombe, Hastingleigh, near Ashford, Kent.

Pilot: Gefr Hubert Rungen, who was captured.

The Bf 109 started out from near Boulogne at 1325 hrs escorting 109 Jabo bombers to the Thames, east of London. The formation was about 60 strong and included the whole of III./JG 3. When at 27,000ft over London, the formation was attacked by about ten Spitfires and Rungen's aircraft got separated from the others. He attacked two Spitfires but a third climbed from underneath and shot his plane through the radiator. Making for the coast, being chased by the Spitfire, he eventually force-landed. Only seven .303 strikes were found in the aircraft but some of these were in the radiator and the engine overheated.

Markings: white 'I' and '7' with black edging; yellow nose and rudder; green spinner and blades. The aircraft was fitted with a bomb release gear.

Rungen's Bf 109 was put on public display at various places. The large gothic building is London's Guildhall (see above).

17 October 1940 at approx. 1200 hrs

Messerschmitt Bf 109 E-7 (WNr. 4138), coded 8+, of Stab I./JG 53.

Crashed in the English Channel.

Pilot: Hptm Mayer. His body washed up 10 days later at Littlestone, Kent. He was *Gruppenkommandeur* of I./JG 53 and was thought to have previously been the *Staffelkapitän* of the 1st *Staffel*. He had received rapid promotion and had good career prospects ahead. He served in Spain with the Condor Legion and had gained several awards and decorations. In September 1940 he claimed 20 victories and was awarded the Ritterkreuz.

Markings: white '8'.

25 October 1940 at 0930 hrs

Messerschmitt Bf 109 E-4 (WNr. 1988), coded 7+, of 5./JG 54.

Belly landed at Scotney Court Farm, Broom Hill near Lydd, Kent.

Pilot: Olt Joachim Schypek (see below left).

The Bf 109 started out at 0840 hrs escorting Jabo fighter-bombers to London. There was a large number of aircraft on this operation. Before reaching the objective, Schypek got separated from the rest of the aircraft over Biggin Hill at 26,000ft. He was attacked from both sides by ten Spitfires which he successfully avoided. However, he was shot by an aircraft from behind. His radiator was hit and many strikes were heard against the armour plate. The victory was ultimately attributed to Fg Off Peter Brown (see below right) of 41 Sqn (Hornchurch).

Markings: black '7'.

25 October 1940 at 1330 hrs

Messerschmitt Bf 109 E-4(WNr. 5104), coded 13+, of 3./JG 77.

Force-landed at Harveys Cross Farm, near Telscombe Cliffs, north of Saltdean, East Sussex.

Pilot: Gefr Karl Raisinger. He was captured unhurt by a local farmer and handed over to the police.

The Bf 109 took off from near Calais at 1230 hrs on bomber escort duties. On the return journey, while flying at 17,000ft over London, the formation was attacked by Spitfires and the aircraft was hit in the radiator. The pilot tried to reach the coast but had to force-land. The starboard side of the engine cowling was burnt out to the level of the spark plugs. The aircraft ended up as a Spitfire Fund exhibition at Rootes car show room in Maidstone, Kent.

Markings: red '13'; yellow cowling with 'Rocho' written on one side in red.

25 October 1940 at 1355 hrs
Messerschmitt Bf 109 E-4 (WNr. 5178), coded 2+, of 5./JG 54.

Belly landed at Lydd Ranges, West of Galloways Road, Dungeness, East Sussex.

Pilot: Lt Ernst Wagner, who was taken prisoner of war.

This was the pilot's second sortie of the day. It started at 1235 hrs, escorting bombers to London. Soon after crossing the coast at 26,000ft Wagner and his *Rottenhund* (wing man) became separated from the rest of the formation by Spitfires. They followed the formation towards London and sighted a squadron of Spitfires below them and, while preparing to attack, they, themselves were attacked by Spitfires from above. Wagner was separated from his *Rottenhund* and dived for thick cloud. When he emerged, he found himself over the sea about 100km south of Hastings. Being lost, he made for the English Coast but ran out of fuel and crash landed. There were no bullet strikes to be seen.

Markings: black '2', outlined in white; yellow upper half of the cowling and orange lower half; green spinner with a white flash and red ring at the tip; yellow rudder.
   On the fuselage of this aircraft was a square black patch prepared to receive a shield. The pilot said this was to be a man carrying a ladder, riding on a pig.

Armament: two MG 17s and two 20mm cannons. No ammunition had been used and the gun barrel ends were covered in grease-proof paper.

Armour: A cross bulkhead in the fuselage and a plate behind the pilot's head, but there was no curved head protection fitted.

27 October 1940 at 0915hrs

Messerschmitt Bf 109E-4 (WNr. 3525), coded 4+, of 3./JG 52.

Landed at RAF Penshurst (Emergency Landing Ground), near Tonbridge, Kent.

Pilot: Fw Lothar Schieverhöfer.

The aircraft was flying wingman to Olt Ulrich Steinhilper of 3./JG 52 on a freelance sortie to London. The pilot was taken prisoner by Pilot Officer Peter Chesters of 74 Squadron, who had claimed him 15 minutes earlier, having attacked him out of the sun at 23,000ft over RAF Penshurst before landing his Spitfire Mk II (ZP-R) on the airfield.

Assisting RAF 49 Maintenance Unit, Brighton contractor A V Nicholls & Co. appear fully loaded with the downed aircraft en route to the salvage unit at Faygate near Horsham. The two operatives are Jack Austin and a local Brighton man, Bob Sawyer, in his younger days (no cap), who told the author that they had just stopped off at the Swan pub on Park Street, Falmer (formerly the main Lewes Road).

Markings: orange '4'.

27 October 1940 at 0940 hrs

Messerschmitt Bf 109 E-1 (WNr. 3576), coded 13+, of 7./JG 54.

Came down on the beach near Lydd Water Tower, Kent.

Pilot: Uffz Arno Zimmermann, who was taken prisoner of war.

The aircraft was hit in the engine by a burst of gunfire from a
Hurricane during a freelance patrol over London. The damage caused
the engine to malfunction and overheat. The pilot stood no chance
of making it back across the English Channel to his French base at
Guines, especially when the cockpit also filled with smoke.

27 October 1940 at 1800 hrs

Junkers Ju 88 A-5 (WNr. 6129), coded 5J+ER, of 7./KG 4.

Belly landed at Richmond Farm, Duggleby, Malton, Yorkshire:

The Ju 88 started out from Holland at 1600 hrs
to attack aerodromes in Yorkshire. Nine aircraft
of this *Staffel* took part in this raid. They split up
into three *Ketten* to attack Driffield, Dishforth and
Leconfield aerodromes and dived out of low cloud
to attack with bombs and machine guns from a
height of 500ft. This aircraft was brought down by
light AA fire which put the starboard engine out
of action. The pilot made a good belly landing.

Markings: white 'E' and tips of spinners.

Crest: a silver flying bat on a yellow crescent moon.

29 October 1940 at 1715 hrs

Messerschmitt Bf 109 E-4 (WNr. 5153), coded 5+l, of 9./JG 3.

Belly landed at West Court Farm near Wootton Crossroads, Shepherdswell, Kent.

Pilot: Olt Egon Troha, who was captured unhurt.

The pilot, thinking his wingman was protecting his rear, was therefore surprised when attacked by a Spitfire of 74 Squadron, which had closed in on his tail.

Markings: 'battle-axe' emblem of III./JG 3 on each side of the engine cowling along with the name 'Erika', the pilot's individual insignia, in white on the starboard side; 9th *Staffel* 'Seahorse' emblem on the fuselage.

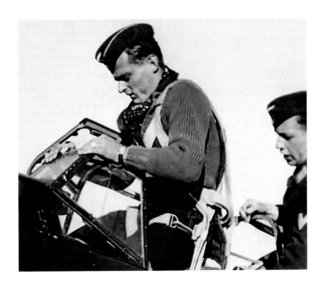

When interrogated, Olt Egon Troha maintained this was not his aircraft and, apart from the *Staffel*'s seahorse crest, all decorations on the machine were purely personal ones of its usual pilot.

Bibliography

Creek, E. J., Mombeek, Eric, Smith, J. R., *Jagdwaffe: Blitzkrieg and Sitzkrieg 1939–1940*, Luftwaffe Colours, Volume One, Section Three (Chevron Publishing, 1999)

Creek, E. J., Mombeek, Eric, Smith, J. R., *Jagdwaffe: Attack in the West 1940*, Luftwaffe Colours, Volume One, Section Four (Chevron Publishing, 2000)

Creek, E. J., Mombeek, Eric, Pegg, Wadman *Jagdwaffe: Battle of Britain* (Phases One and Two), Luftwaffe Colours, Volume Two, Sections One and Two (Chevron Publishing, 2001)

Creek, E. J., Mombeek, Eric, Pegg, Wadman *Jagdwaffe: Battle of Britain* (Phases Three and Four), Luftwaffe Colours, Volume Two, Sections Three and Four (Chevron Publishing, 2002)

Creek, E. J., Smith, J. R., *Kampffliege: Bombers of The Luftwaffe 1933–1940*, Luftwaffe Colours, Volume One (Chevron Publishing/Ian Allan Publishing, 2004)

Creek, E. J., Smith, J. R., *Kampffliege: Bombers of The Luftwaffe 1940–1941*, Luftwaffe Colours, Volume Two (Chevron Publishing/Ian Allan Publishing, 2004)

Goss, Chris, *The Luftwaffe Fighters' Battle of Britain* (Crecy Publishing, 2000)

Goss, Chris, *The Luftwaffe Bombers' Battle of Britain* (Crecy Publishing, 2000)

Ketley, Barry, Rolfe, Mark, *Luftwaffe Emblems 1939–1945* (Hikoki Publications, 1998)

Ketley, Barry, Luftwaffe Emblems 1939–1945 (Flight Recorder Publications, 2012)

Parker, Nigel, Parry, Simon W., *Luftwaffe Crash Archive*, Vols 1–3 (Red Kite, 2013)

Parker, Nigel, Parry, Simon W., *Luftwaffe Crash Archive*, Vols 4–6 (Red Kite, 2014)

Parry, Simon W., *Battle of Britain Combat Archive*, Vols 1–7 (Red Kite, 2015–19)

Parry, Simon W., *War Torn Skies of Great Britain – Surrey in the Battle of Britain* (Red Kite, 2007)

Ramsey, Winston, *Battle of Britain – Then & Now MkV* (After The Battle Press, 1988)

Ramsey, Winston, *The Blitz – Then & Now*, Volume One (After The Battle Press, 1987)

Ramsey, Winston, *The Blitz – Then & Now*, Volume Two (After The Battle Press, 1988)

Smith, J. R., *Stuka: Luftwaffe Ju 87 Dive-Bomber Units 1939–1941*, Luftwaffe Colours, Volume One (Chevron Publishing/Ian Allan Publishing, 2006)

Vasco, John, *Zerstoerer: Luftwaffe Fighter-Bombers and Destroyers 1936–1940*, Luftwaffe Colours, Volume One (Chevron Publishing/Ian Allan Publishing, 2005)

Vasco, John, *The Messerschmitt Bf 110 in Color Profile: 1939–1945* (Schiffer Military History, 2005)

Vasco, John, *Messerschmitt Bf 110 Bombsights Over England: Erprobungsgruppe 210 Fighter Bomber Unit in the Battle of Britain* (Schiffer Military History, 1990)

Vasco, John, Cornwall, Peter, *Zerstoerer: Messerschmitt 110 and Its Units in 1940* (JAC Publications, 1995)